Photographs by **Jack Faragasso**
Edited and Designed by **Carissa Pardee**

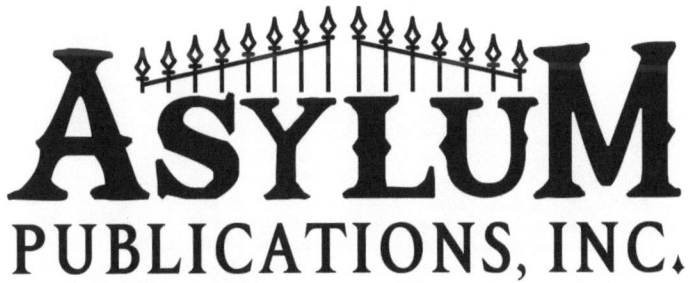

CEO AND EDITOR IN CHIEF **PAUL BURKE**

ISBN: 978-1-7363197-9-6

MODELS Through the Lens of Jack Faragasso™. Published by Asylum Publications, Inc. ™ © by Jack Faragasso. Asylum Publications, Inc. logo TM 2023. All rights reserved. No portion of this publication may be reproduced or transmitted, in any form by any means, without written consent from the Publisher, except for any small excerpts for the purpose of review. For further information regarding custom photo/art books, ordering wholesale, or other inquiries, please write to asylumpublications75@gmail.com.

www.asylumpublications.com

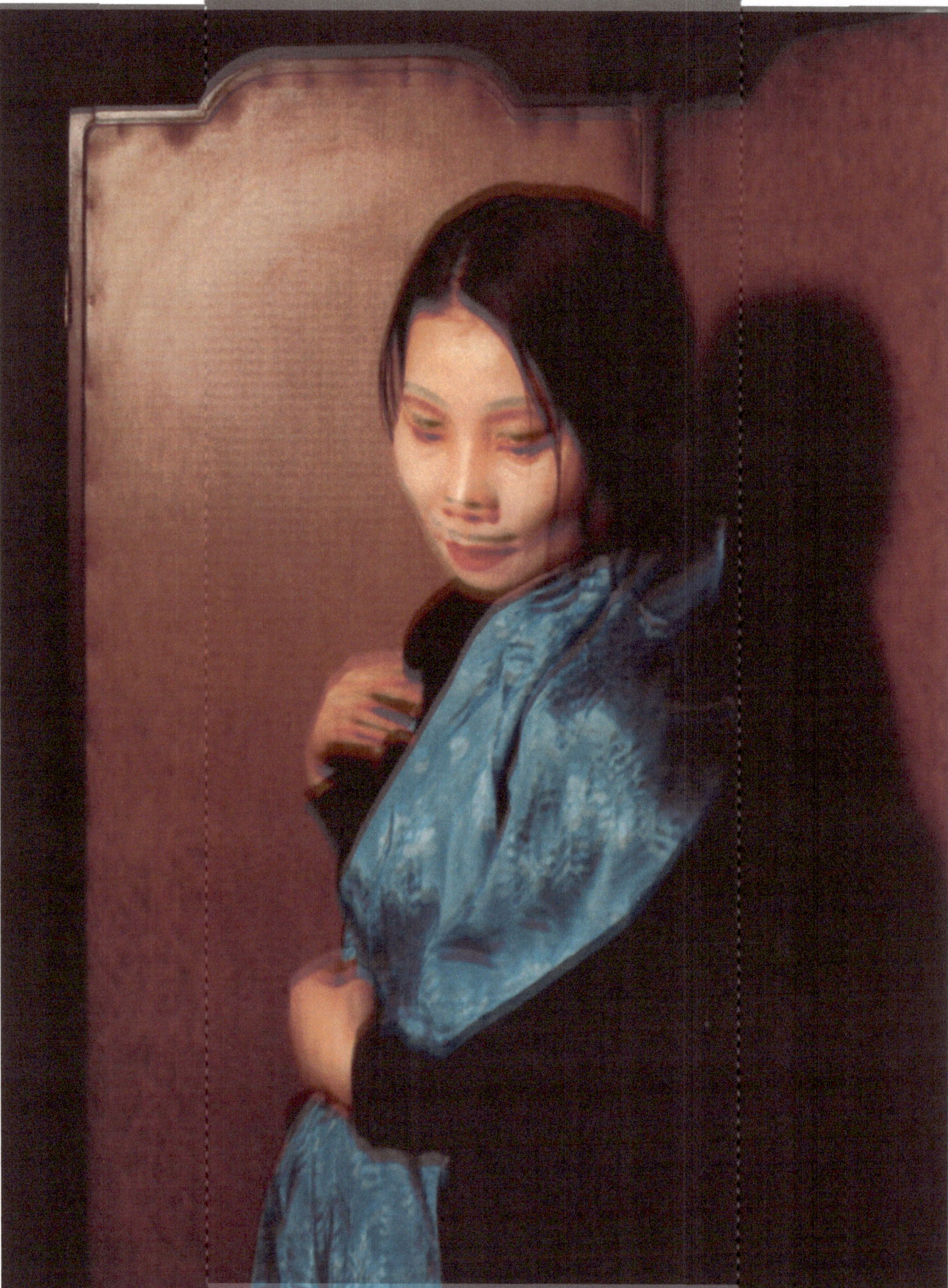

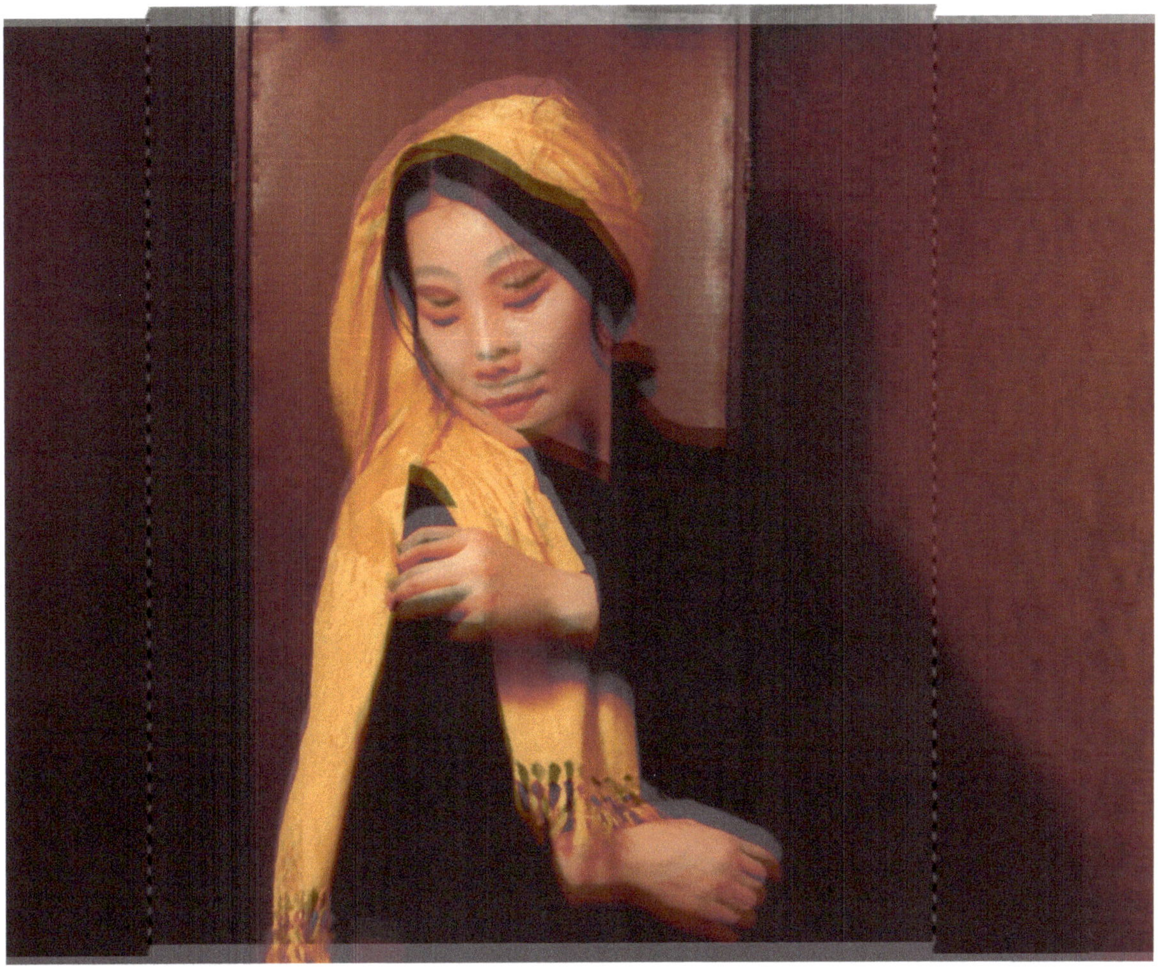

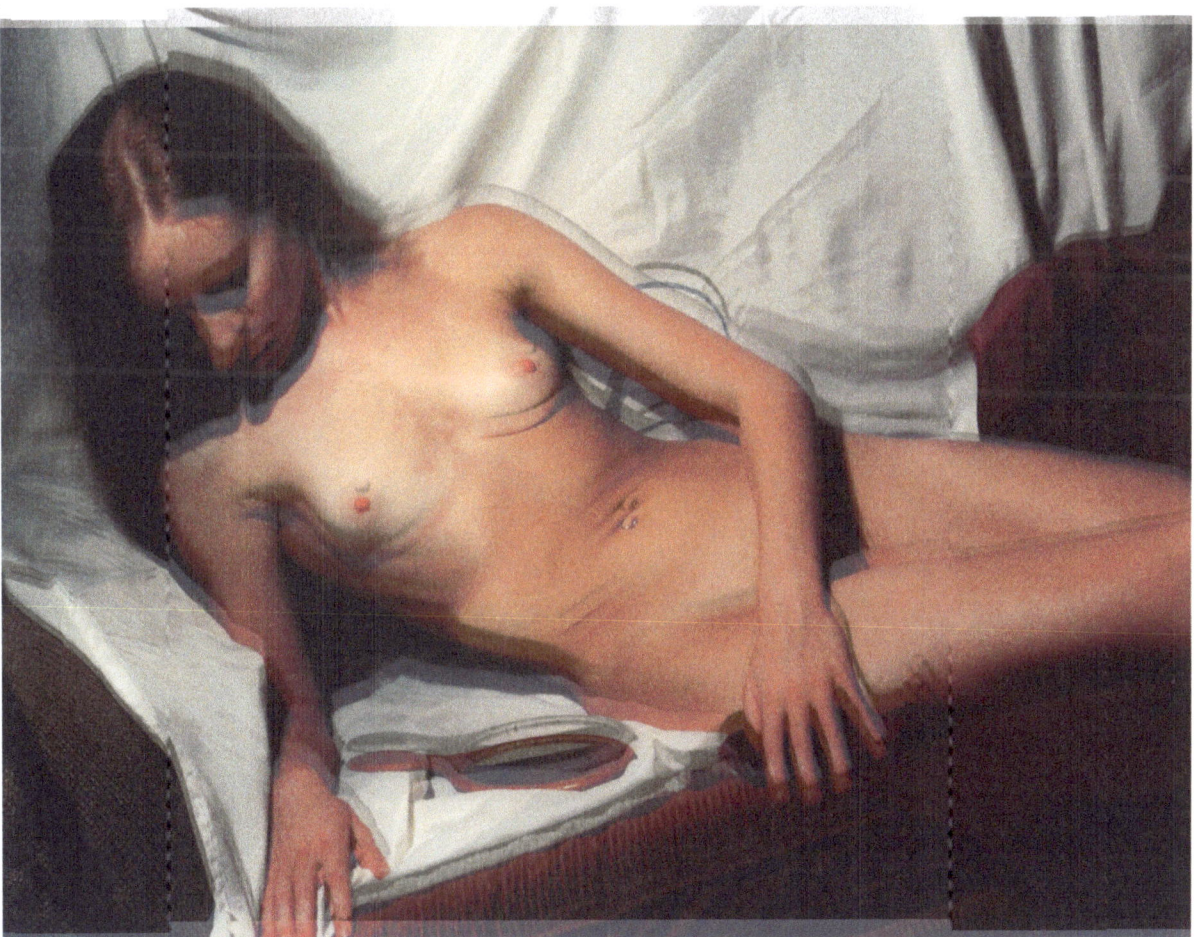

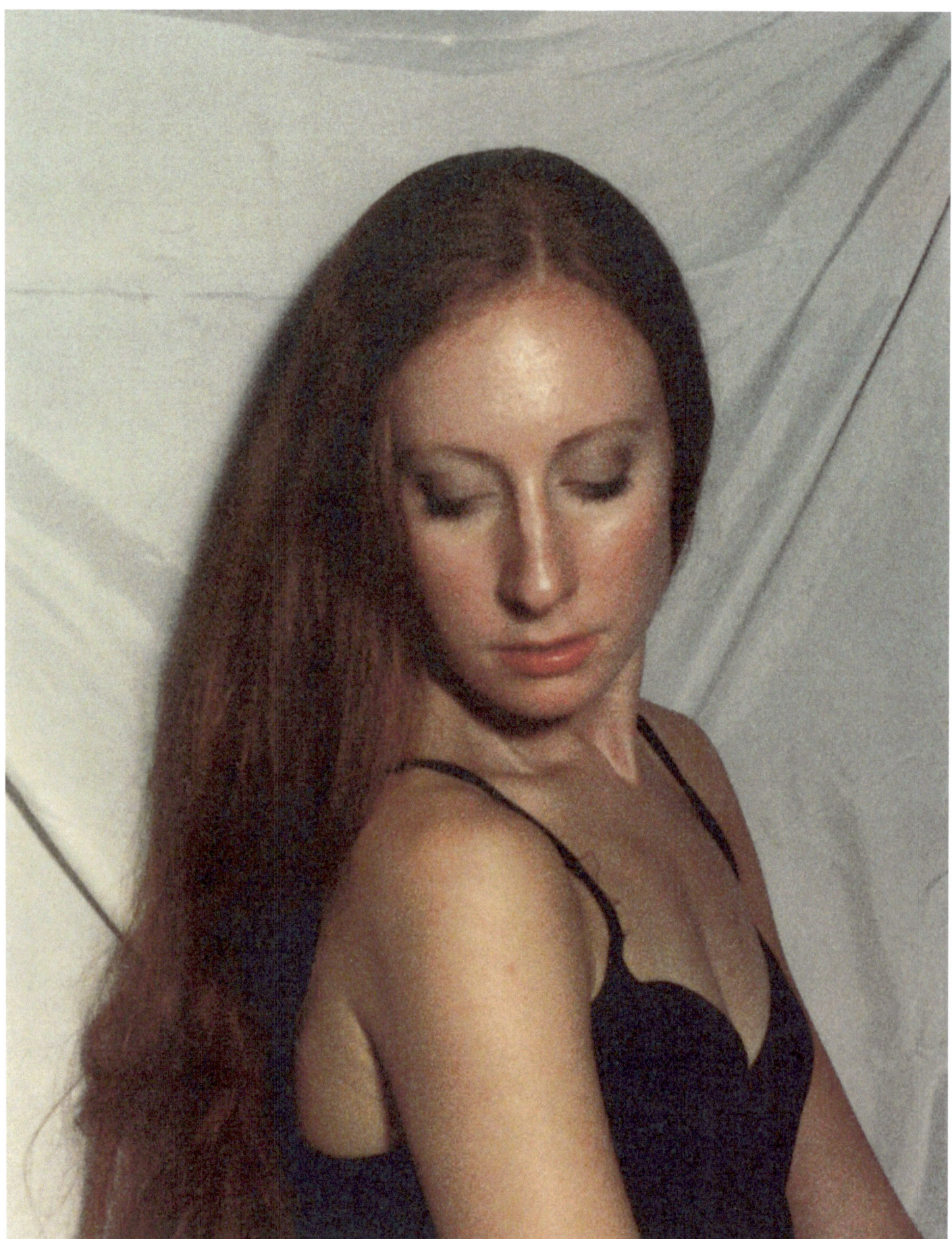

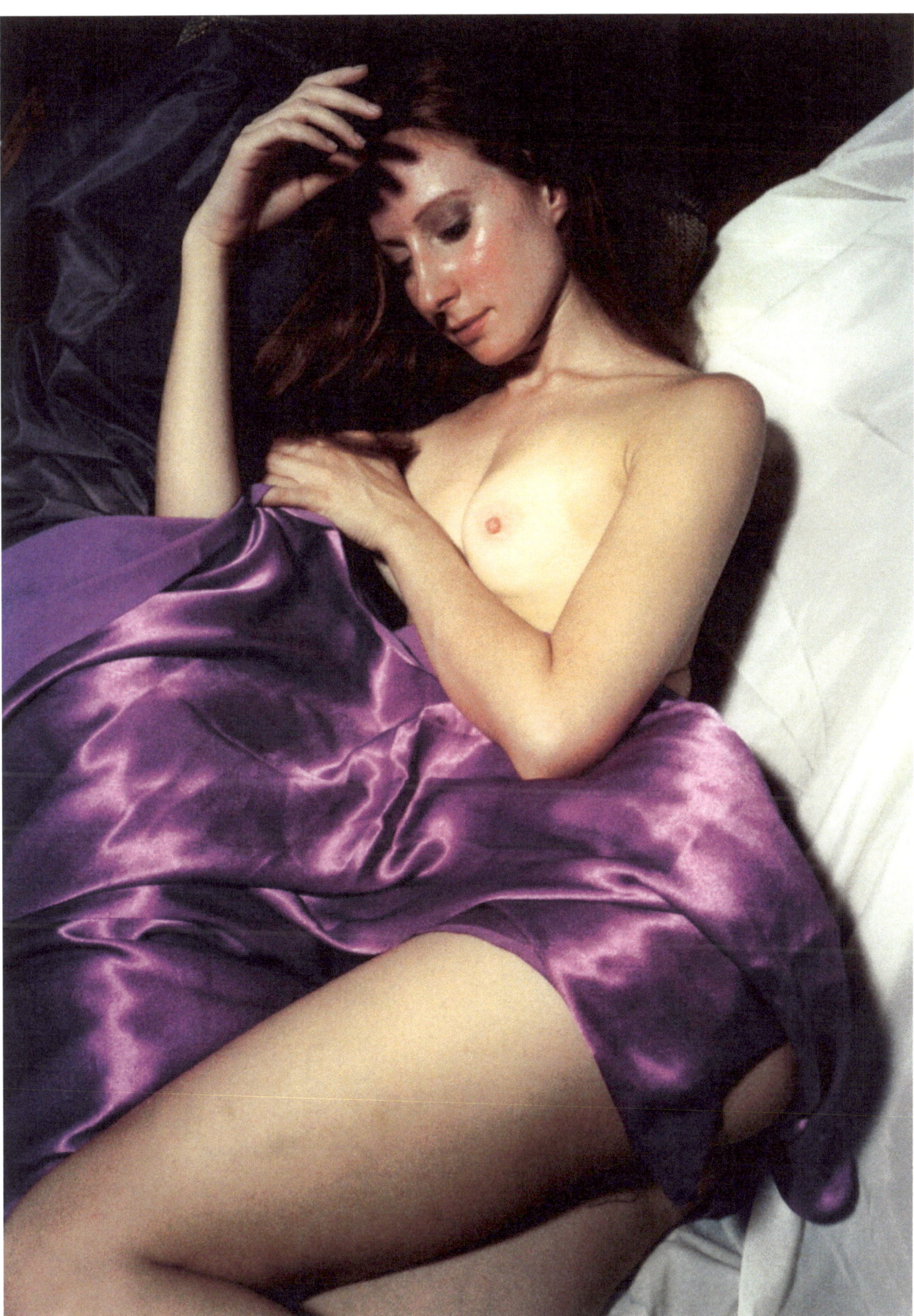

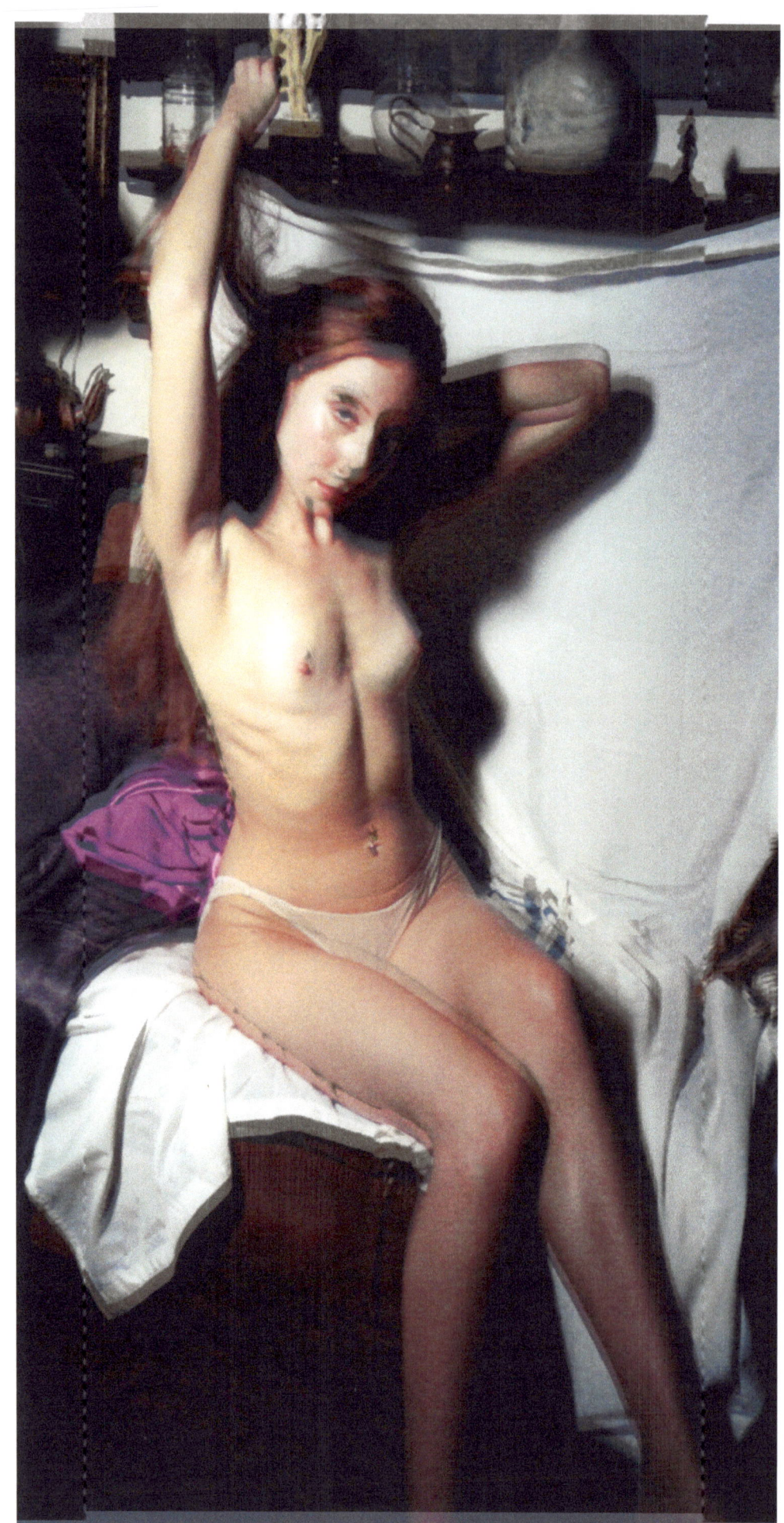

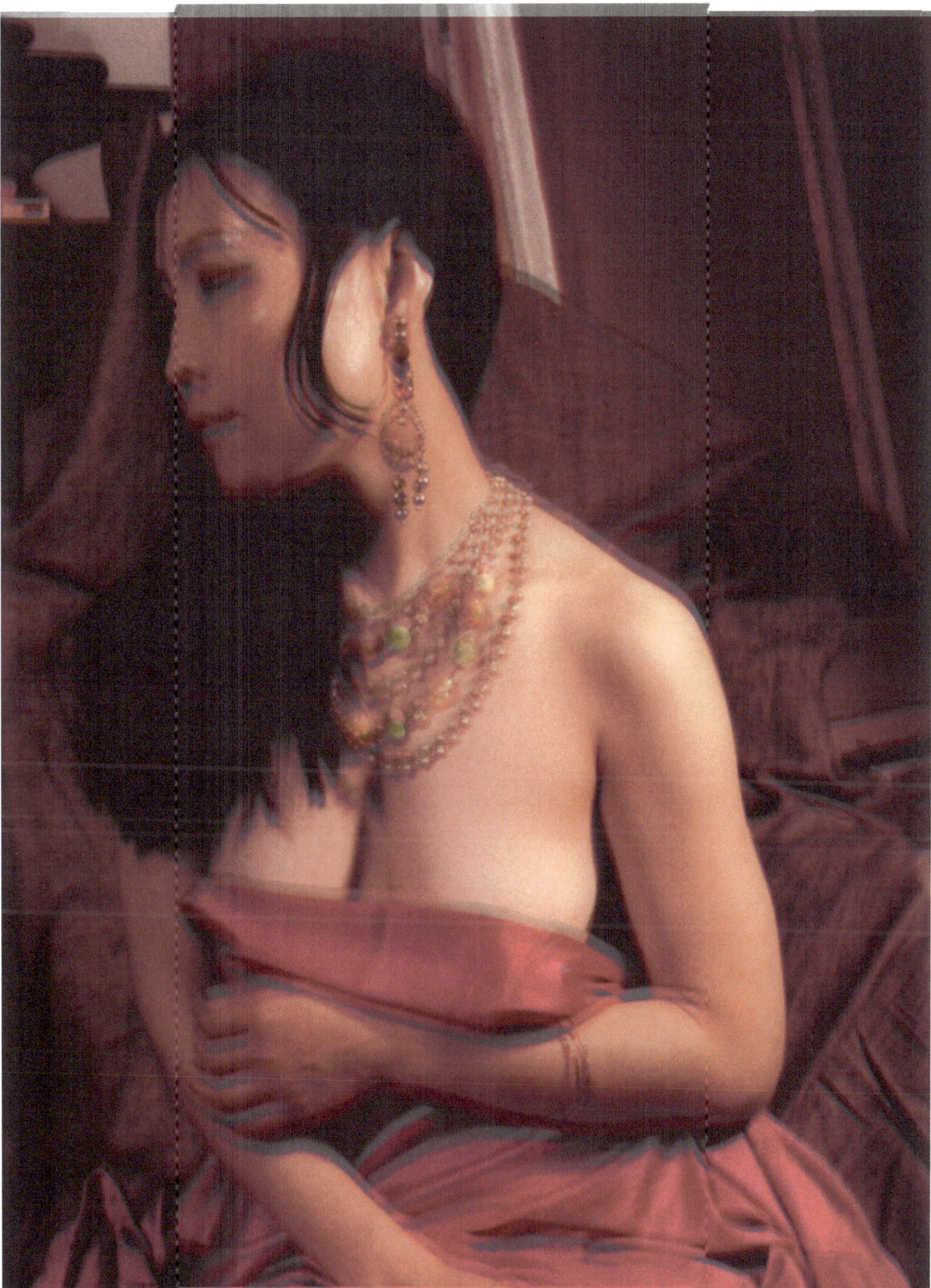

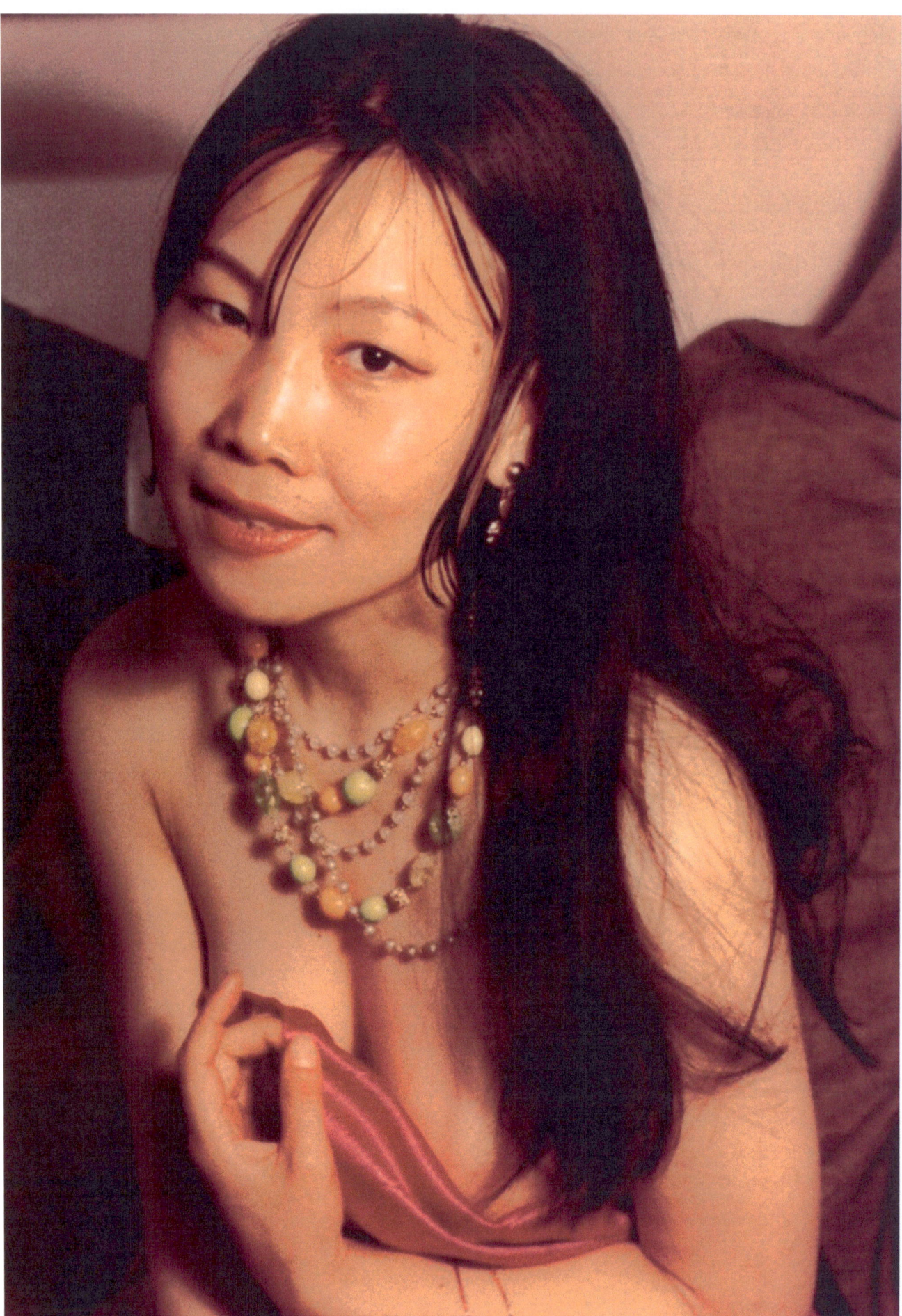

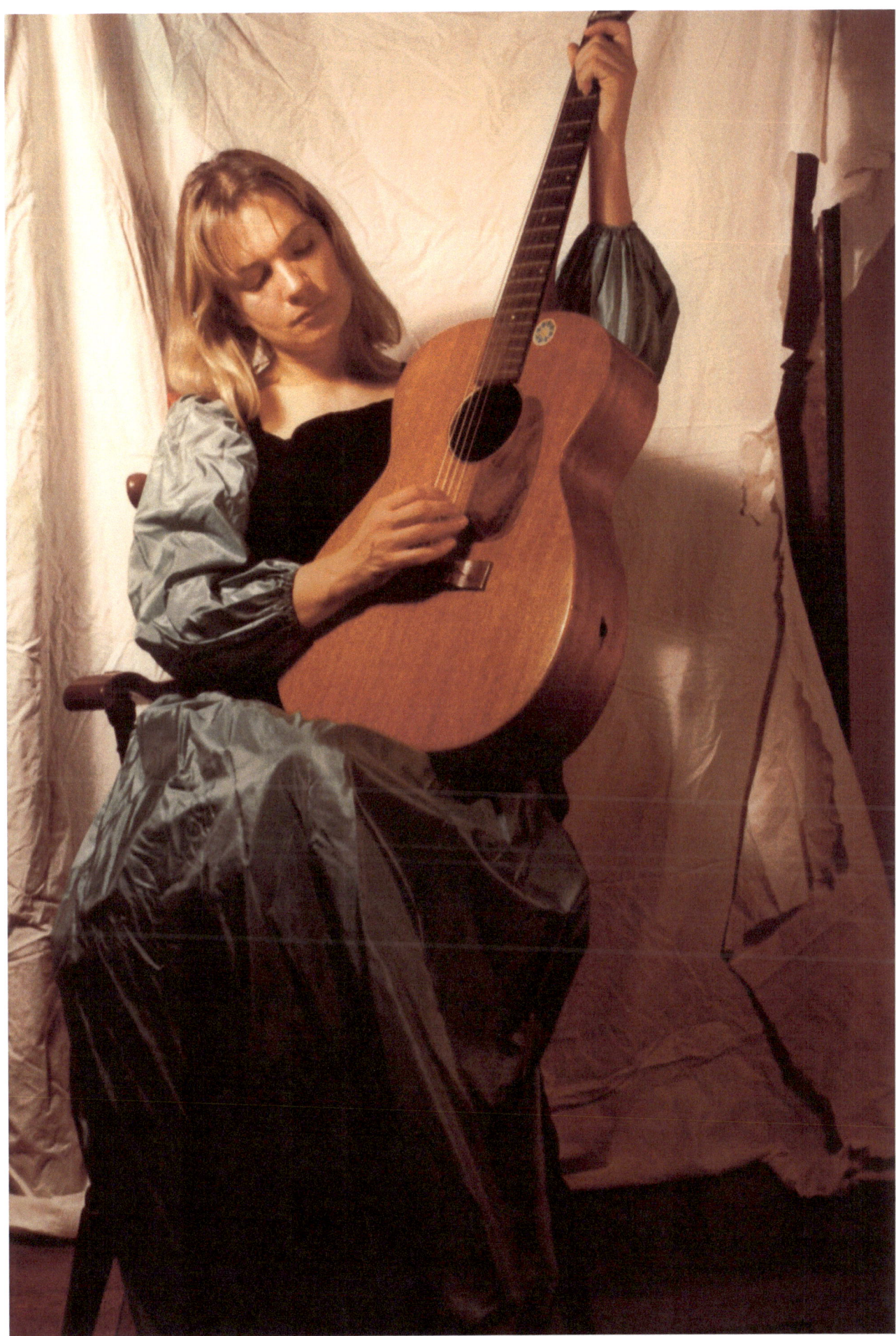

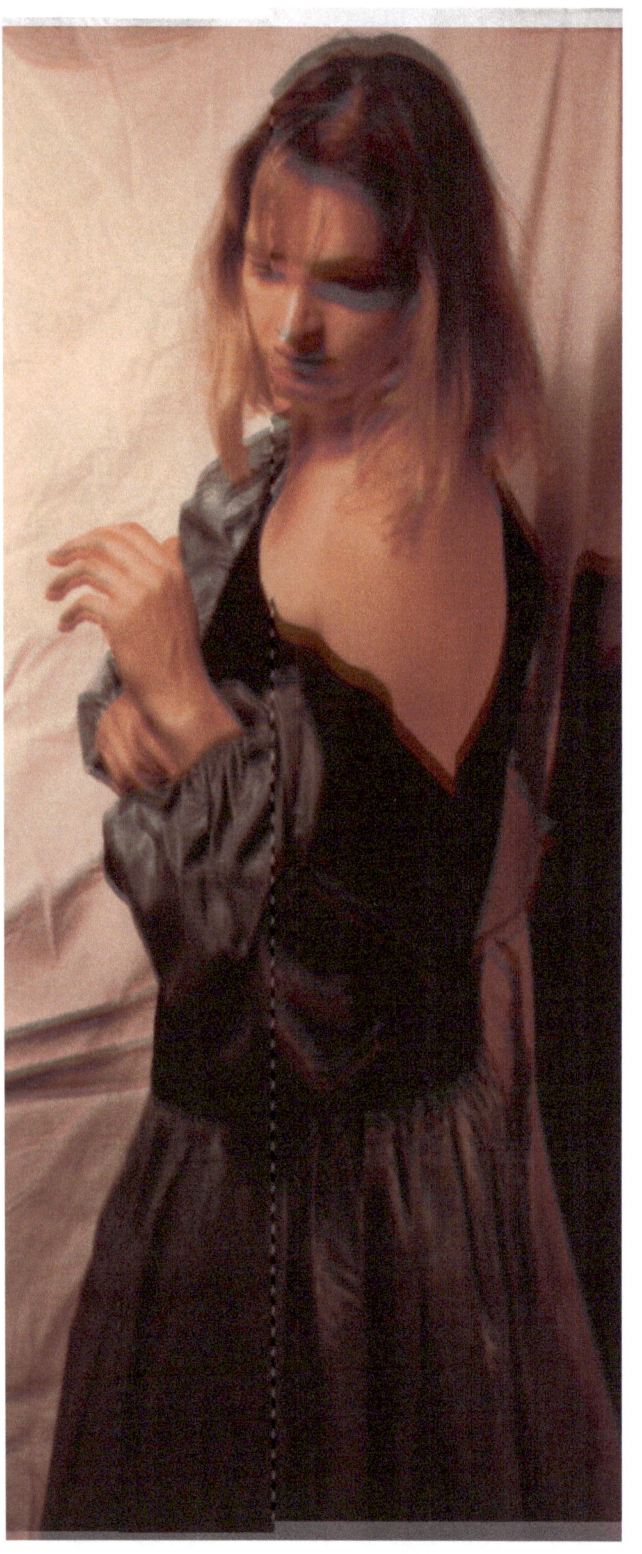
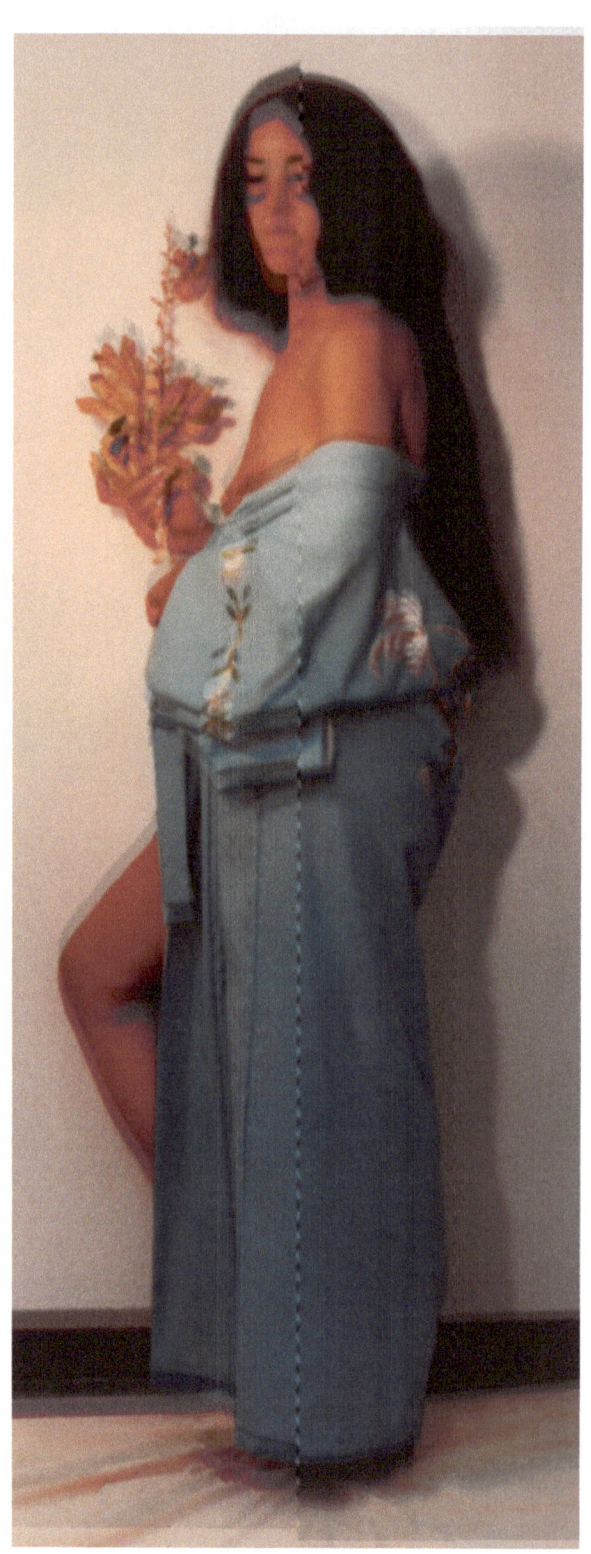

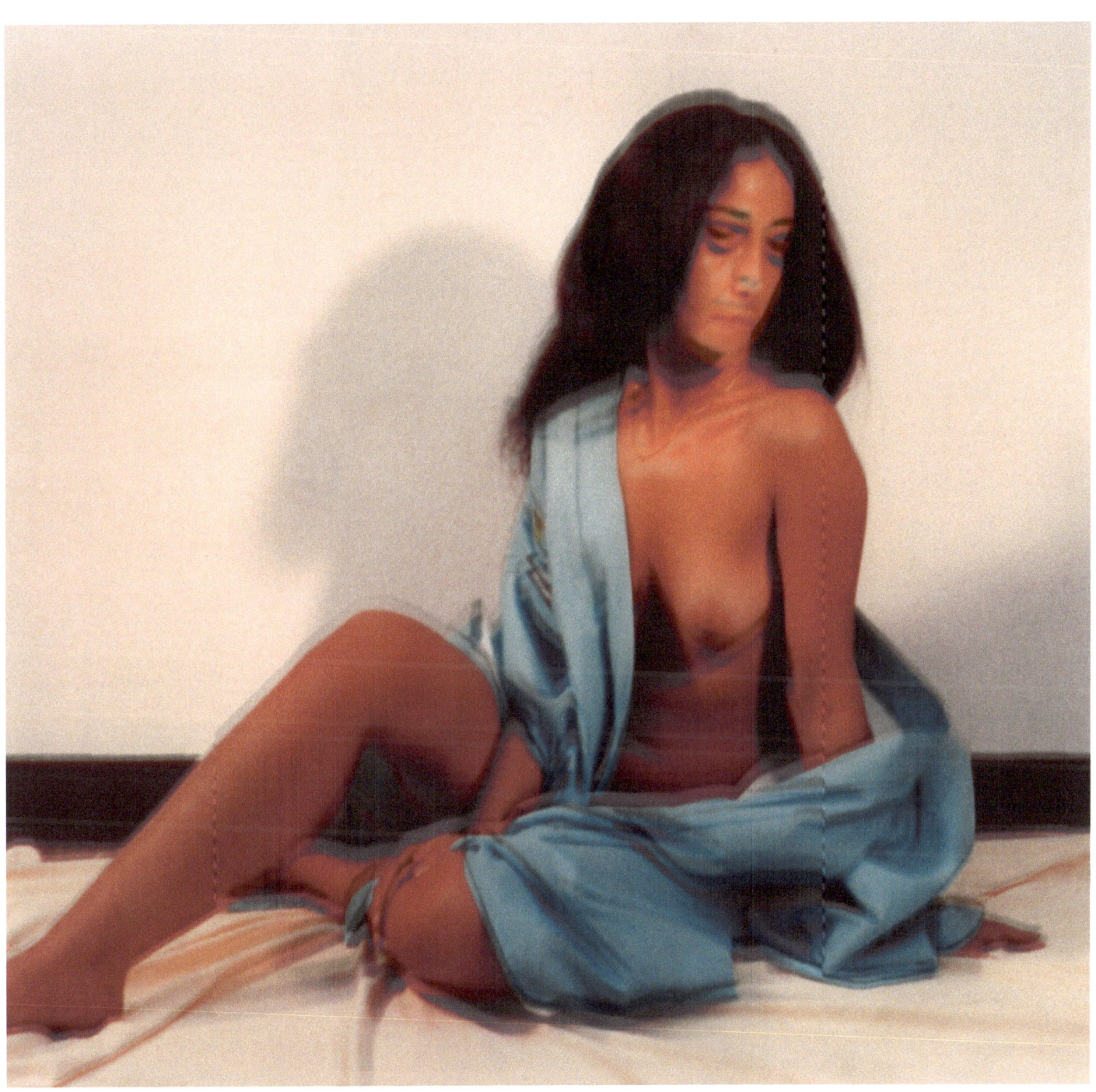

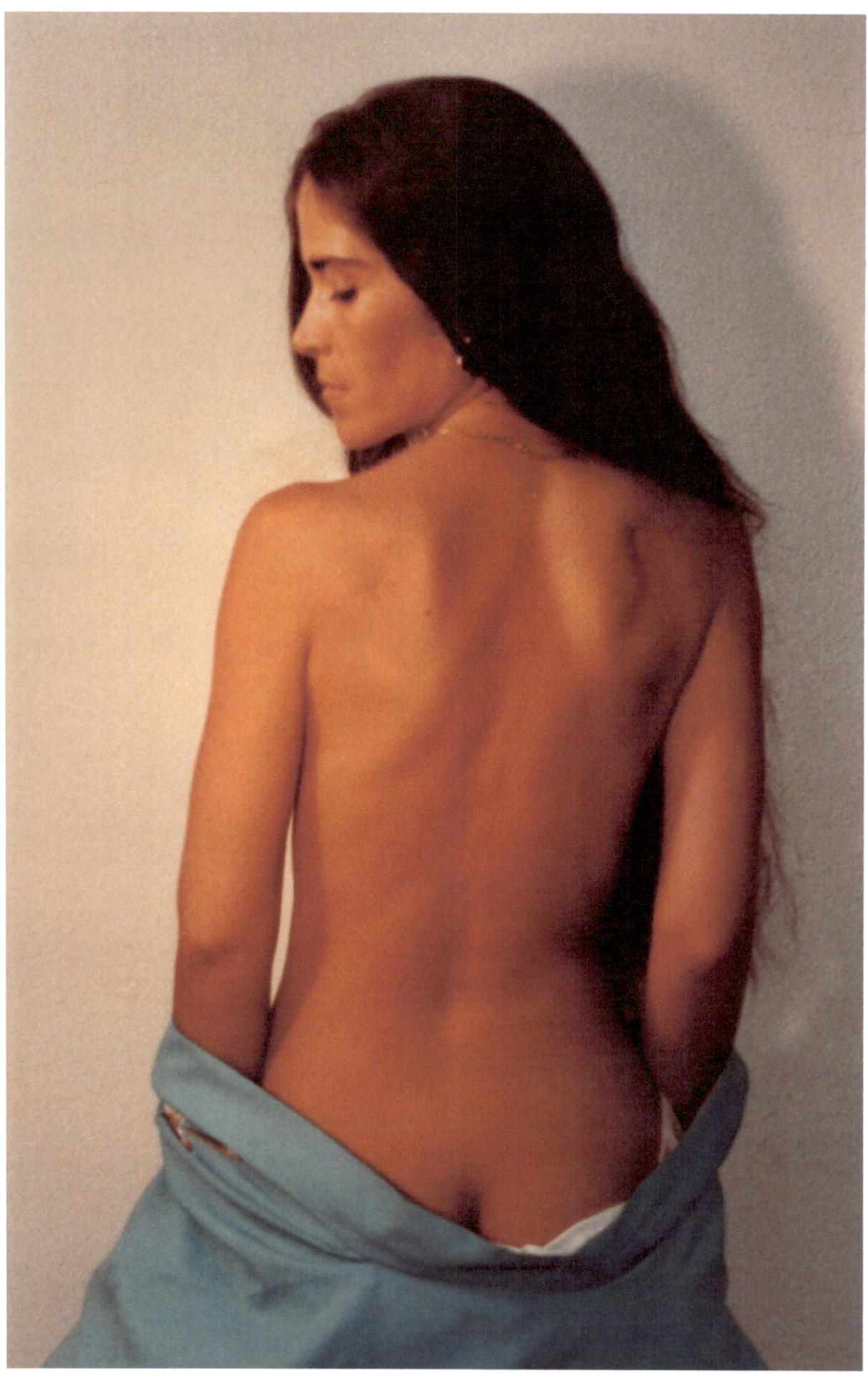

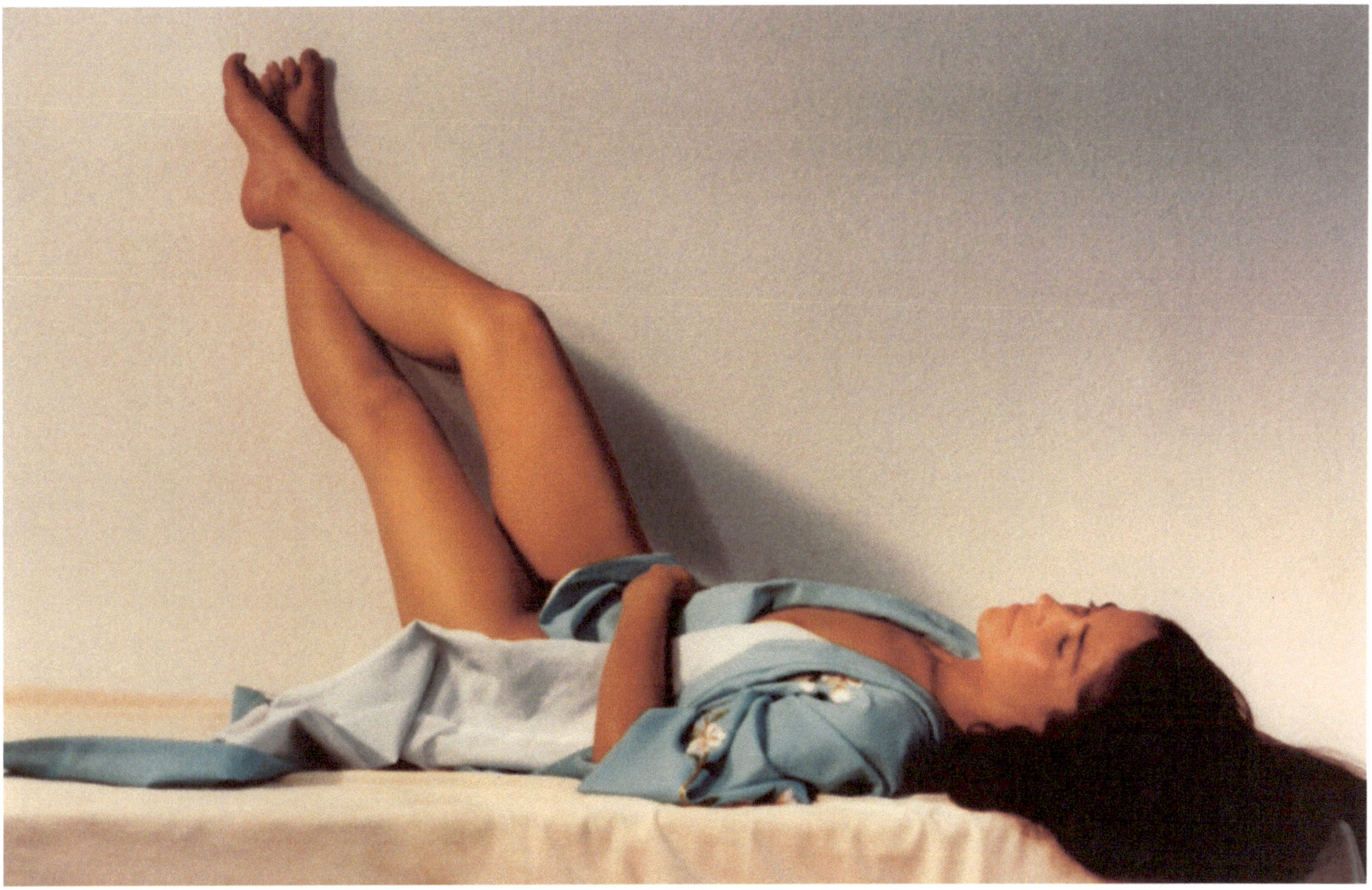

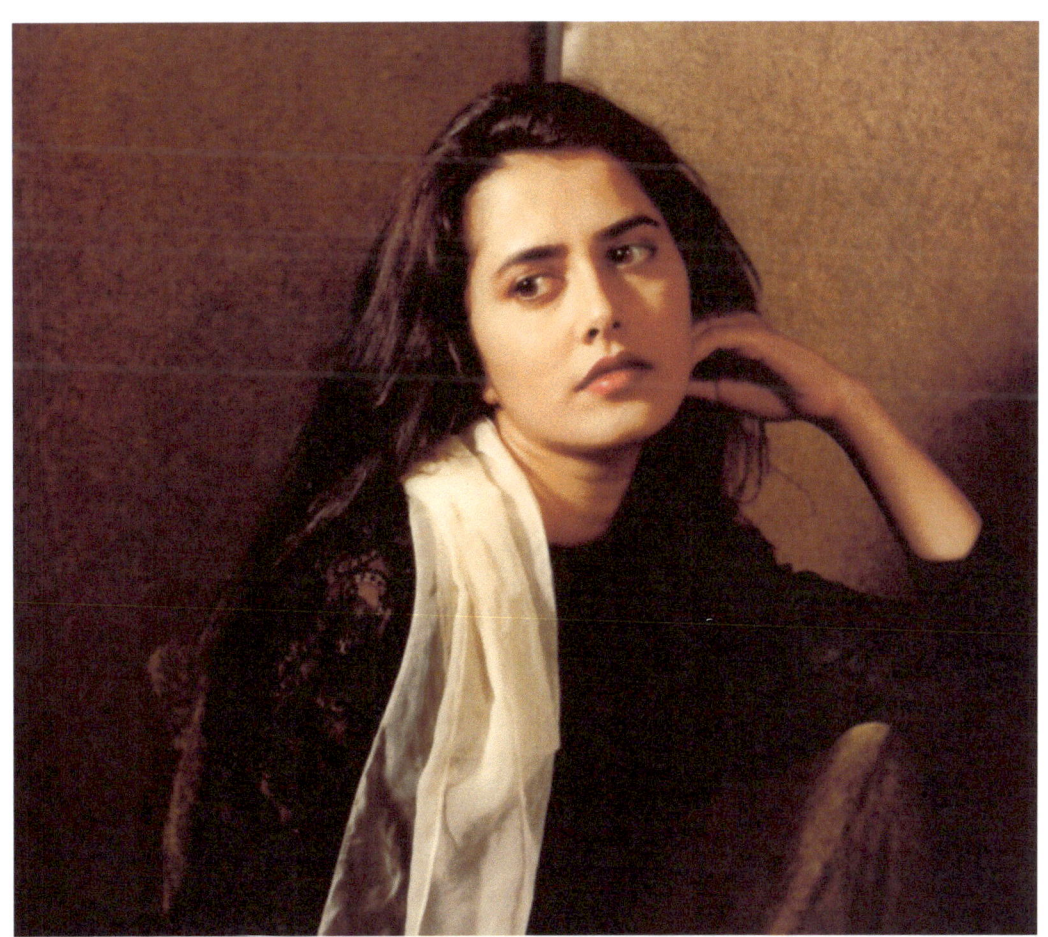

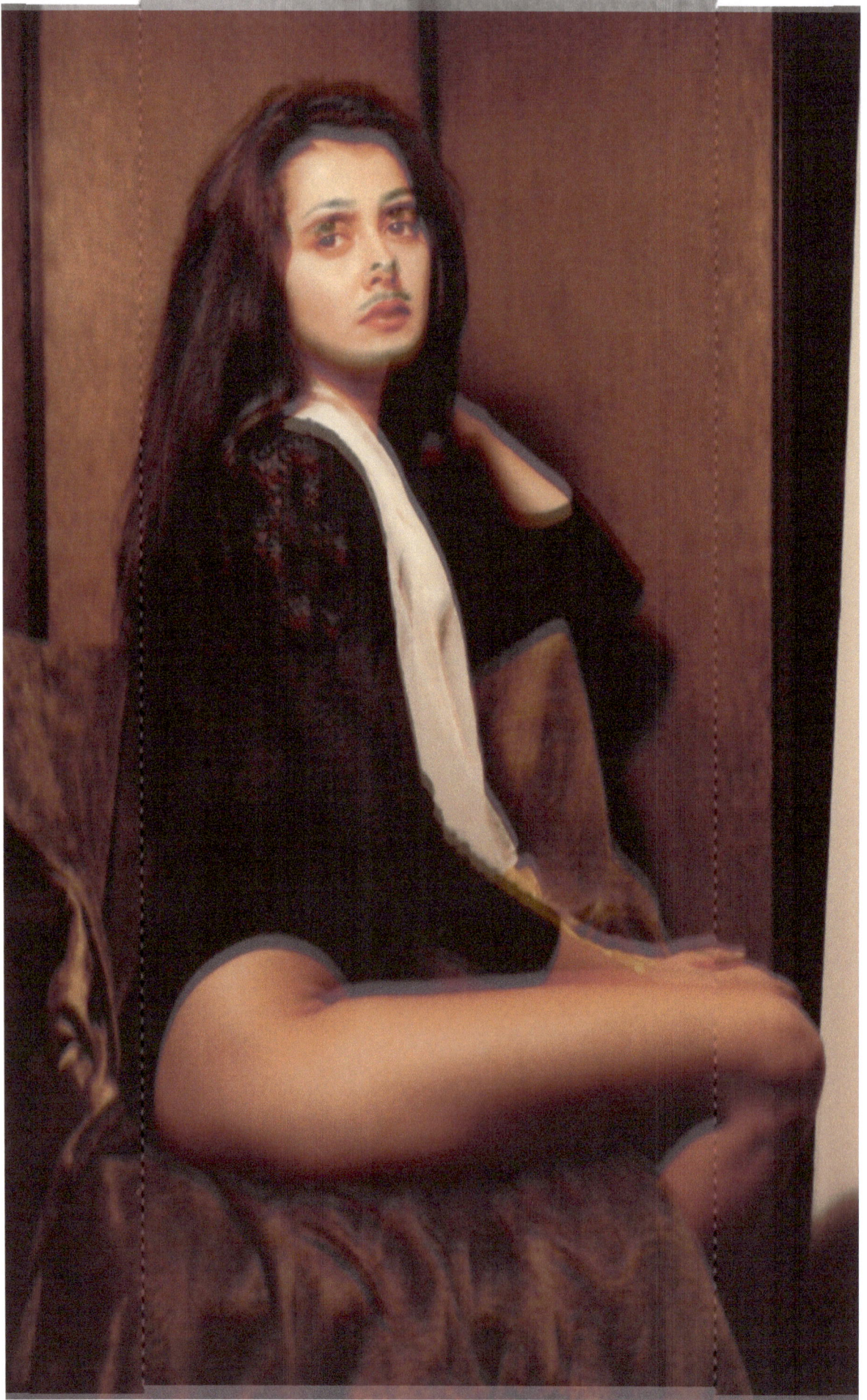

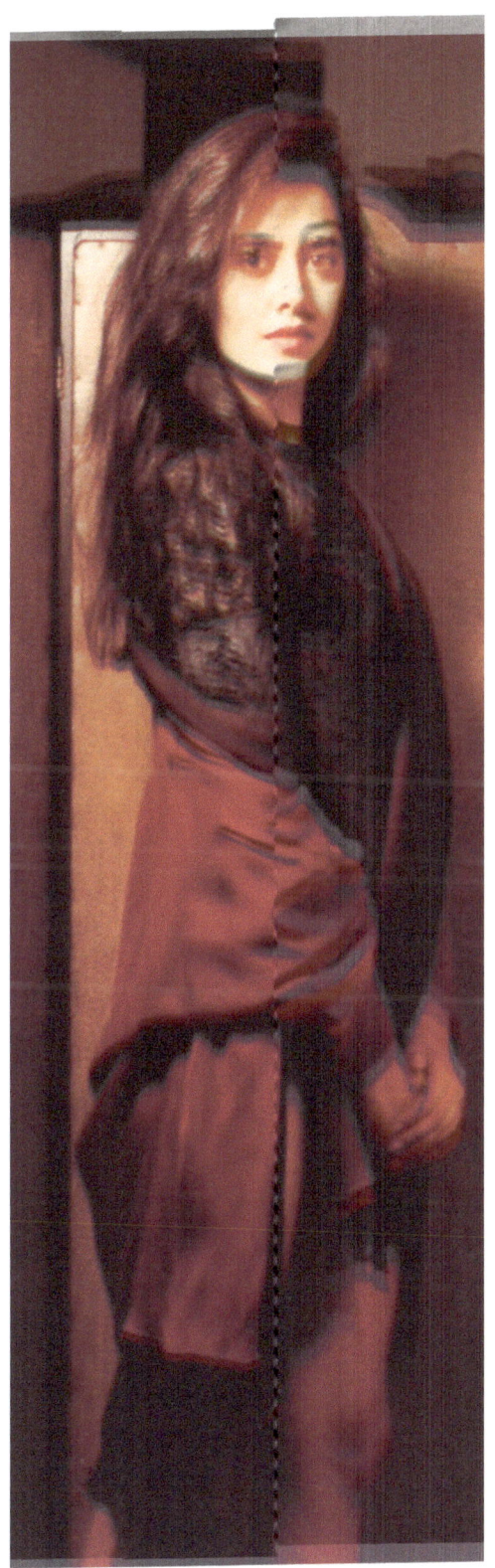
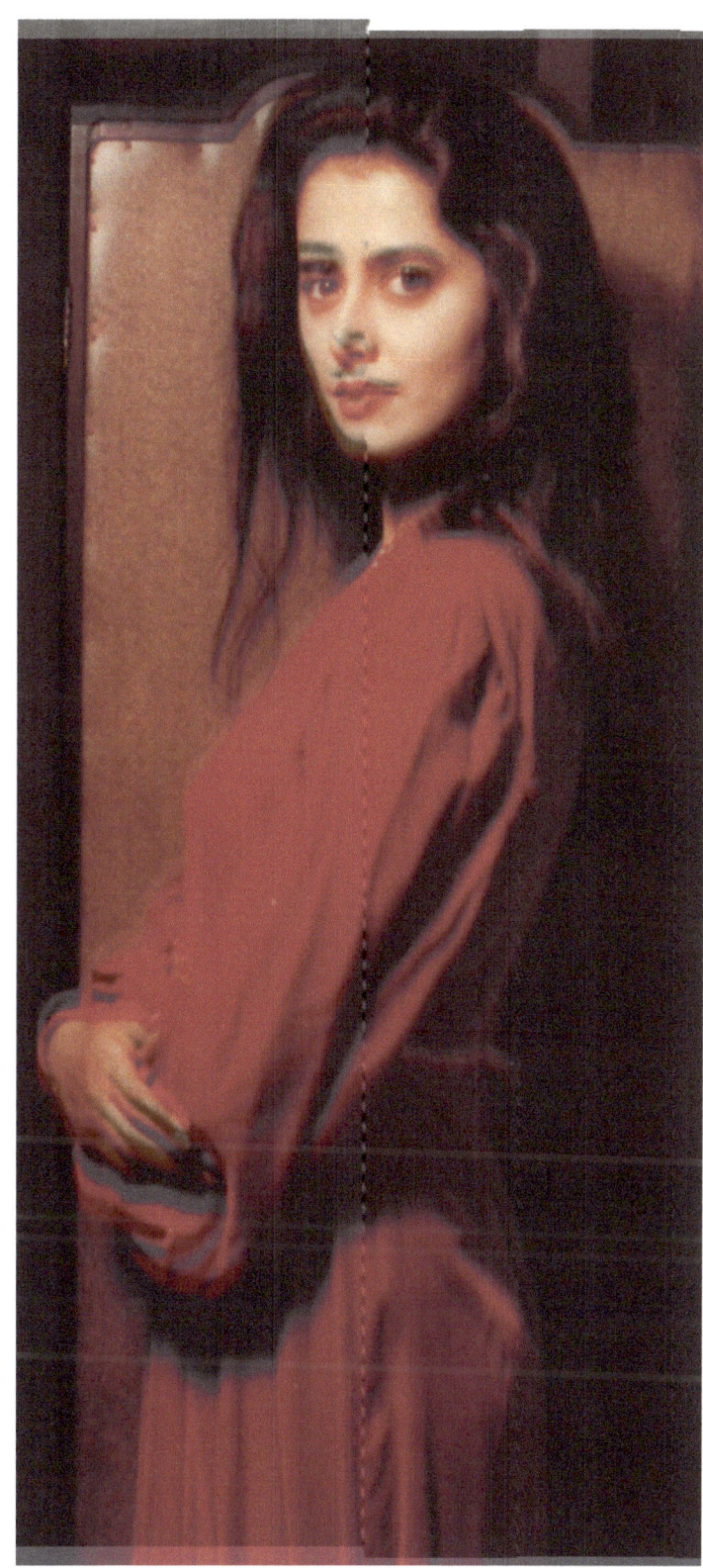

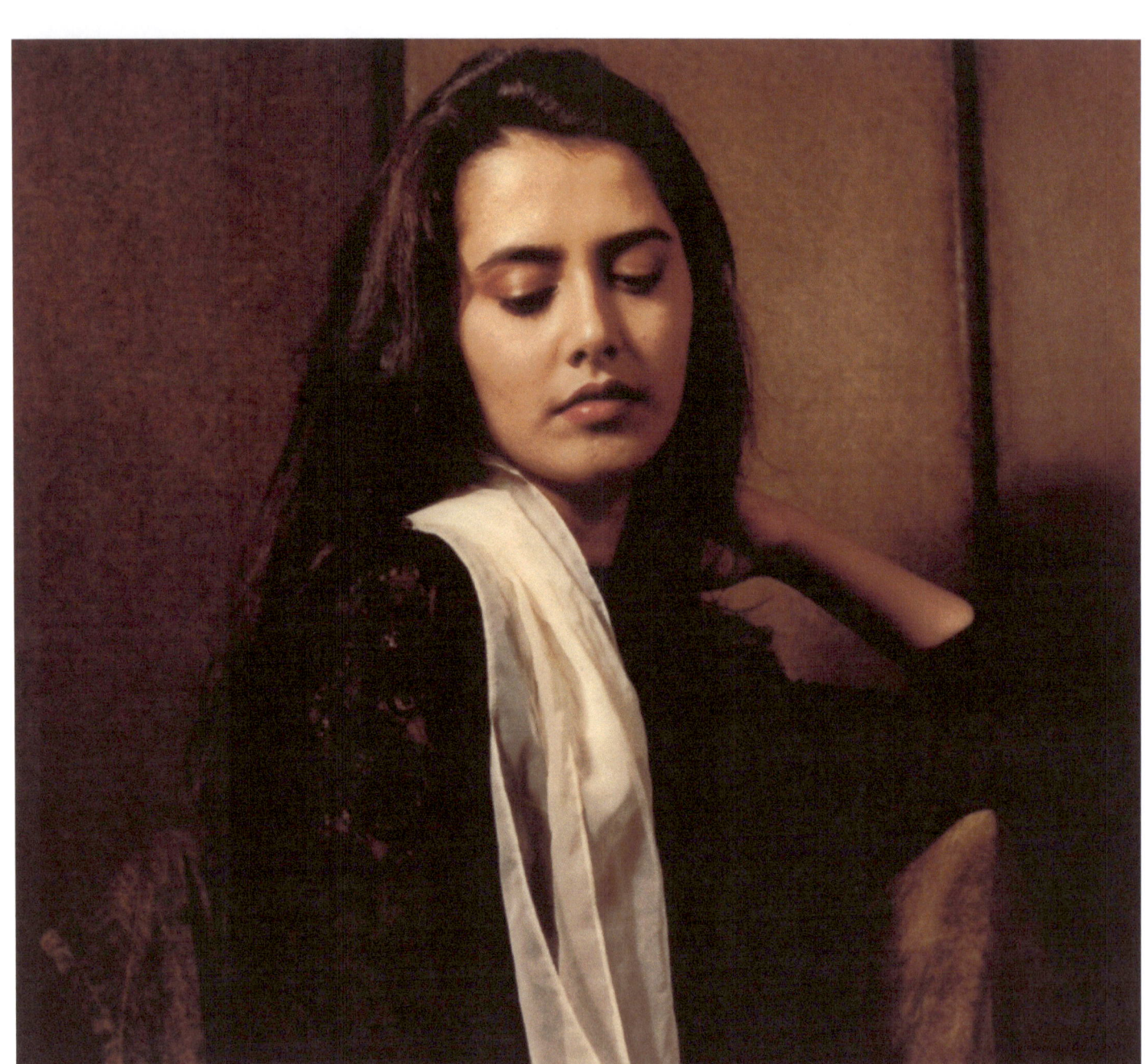

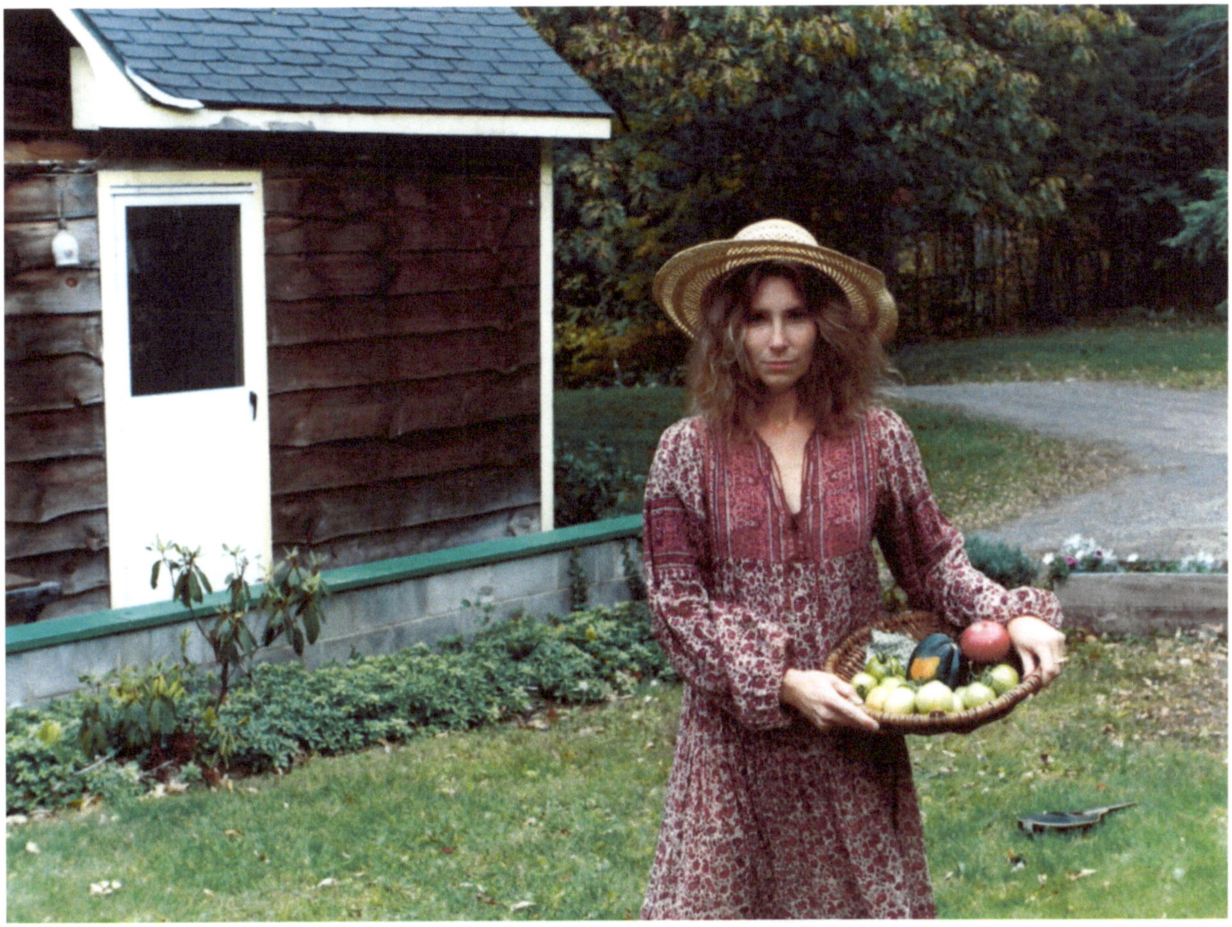

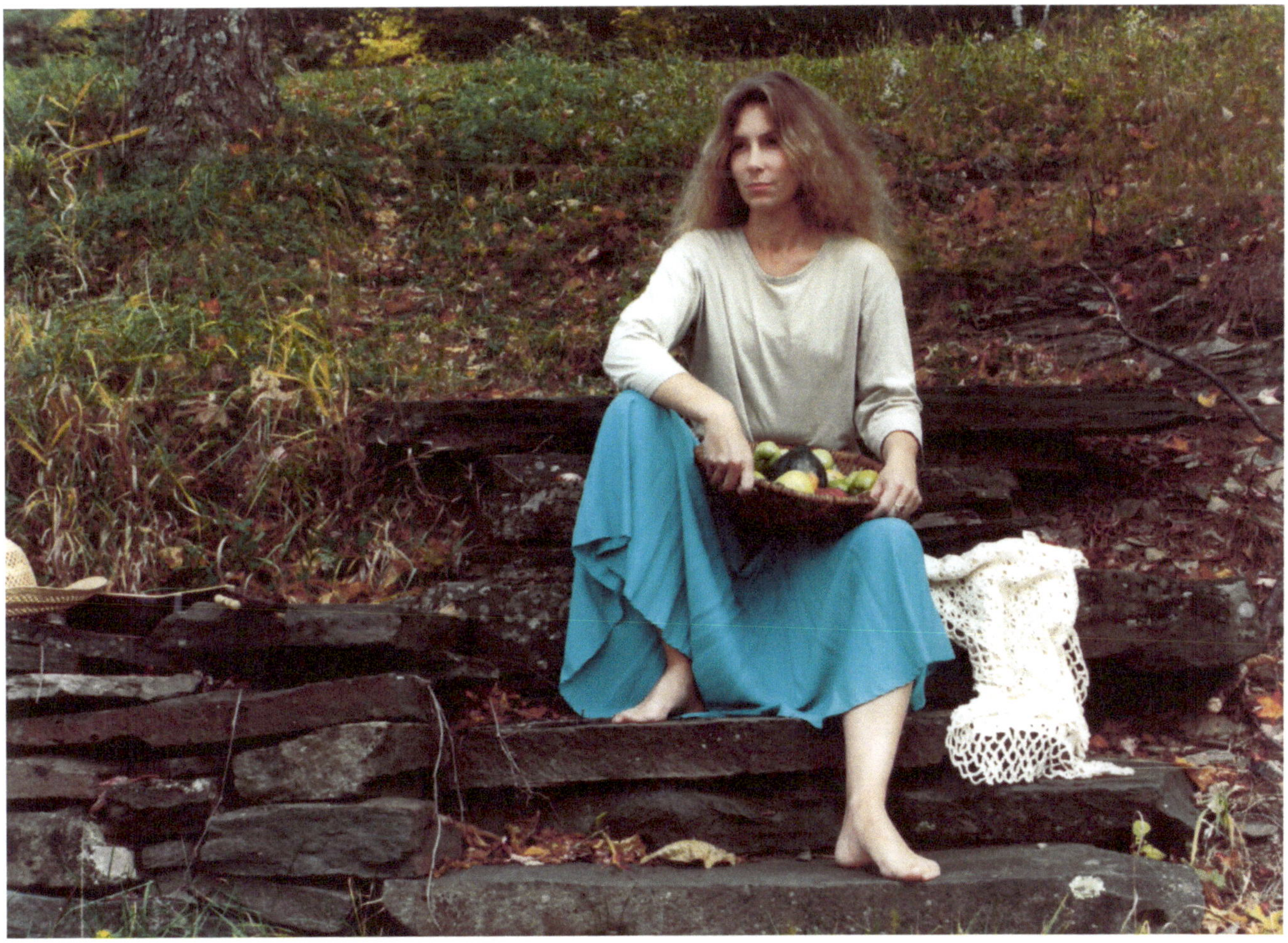

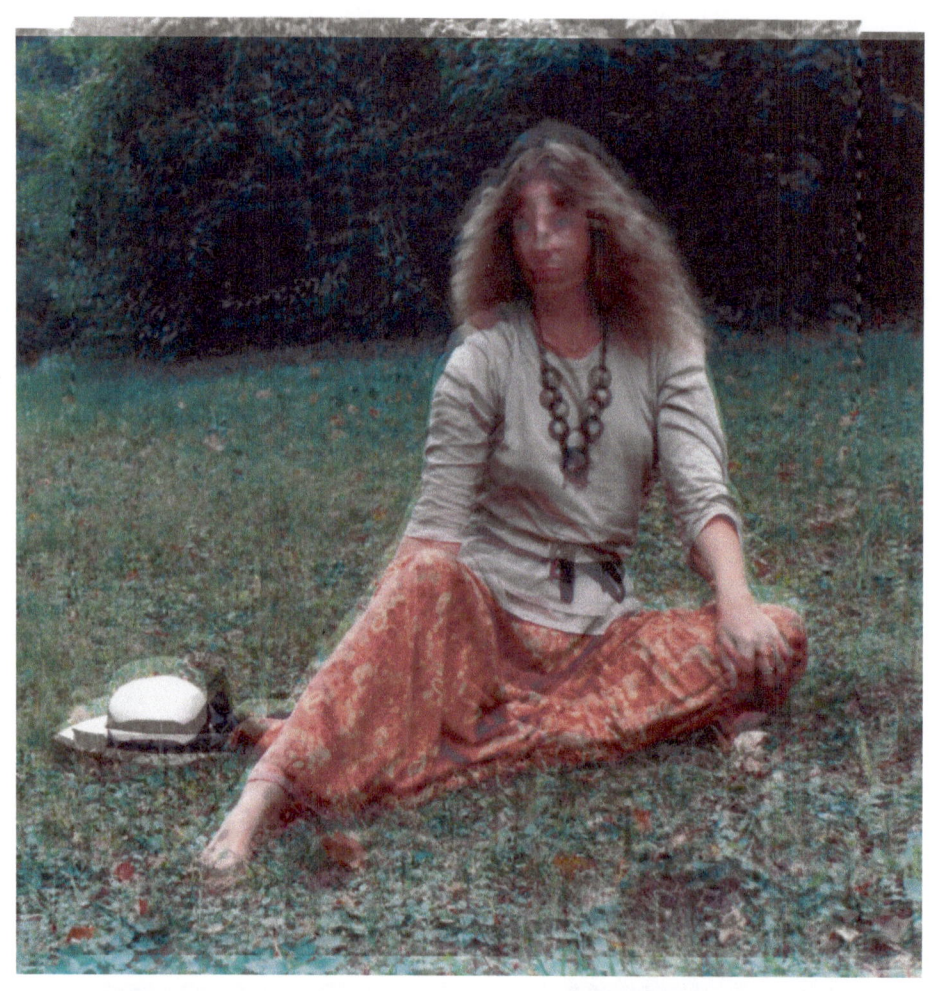

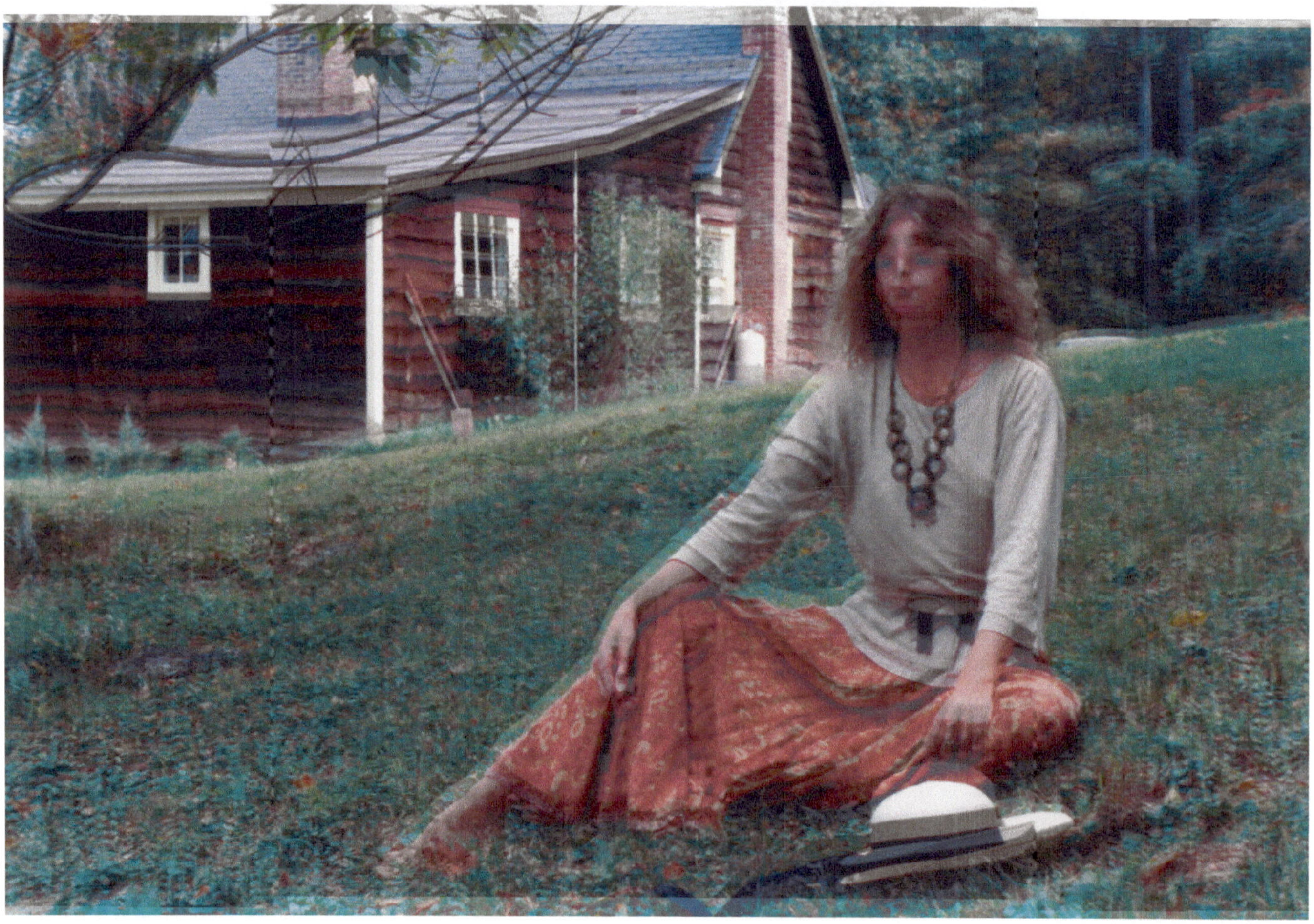

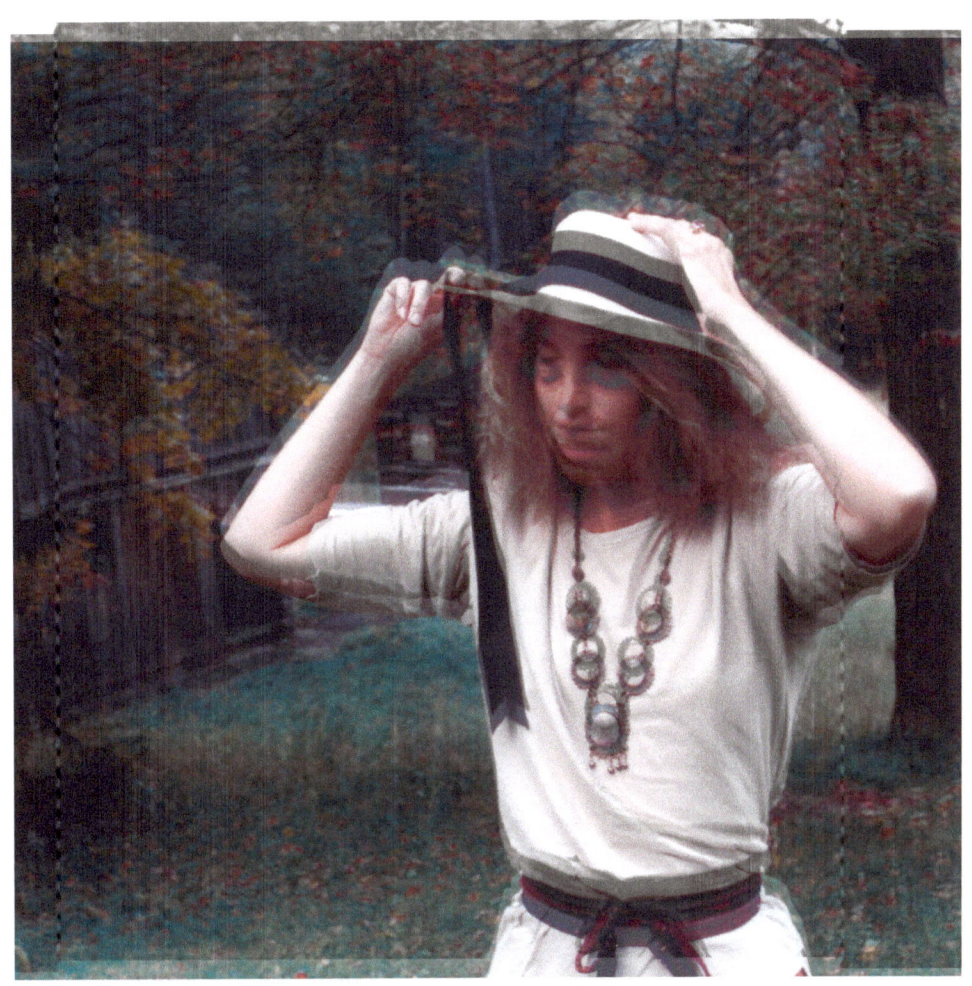
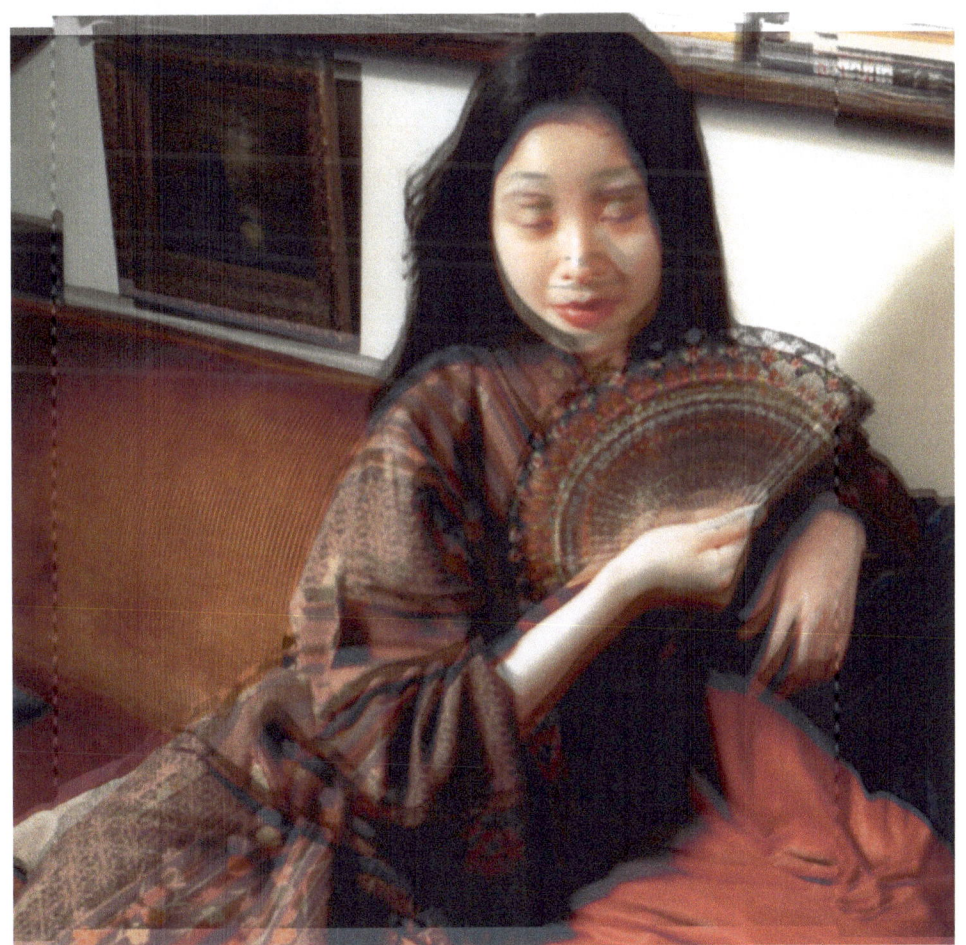

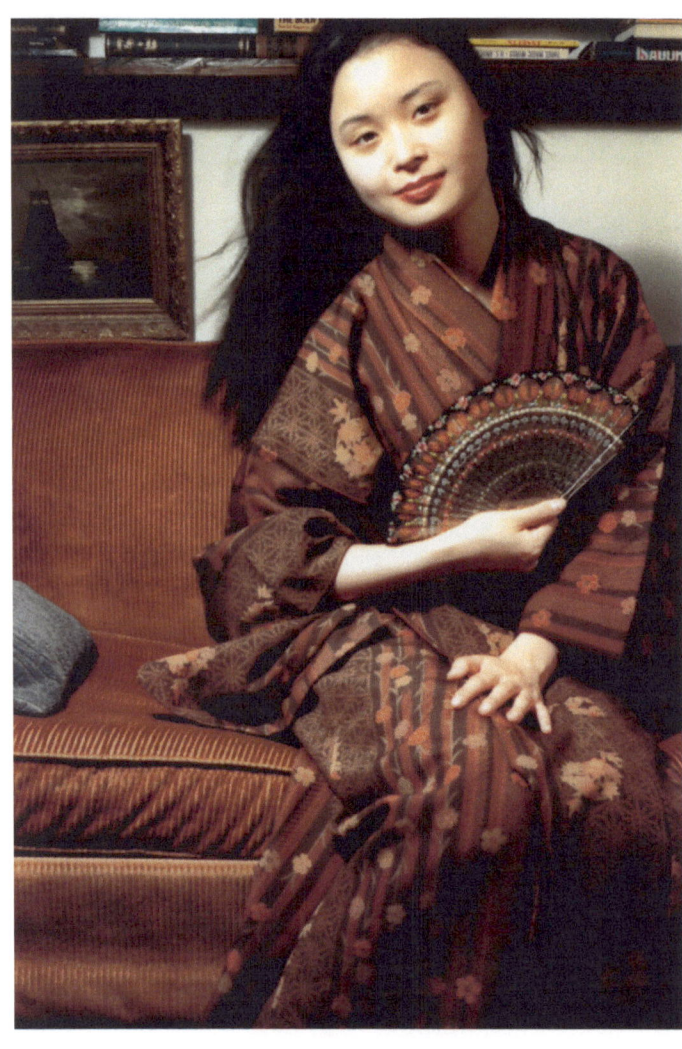
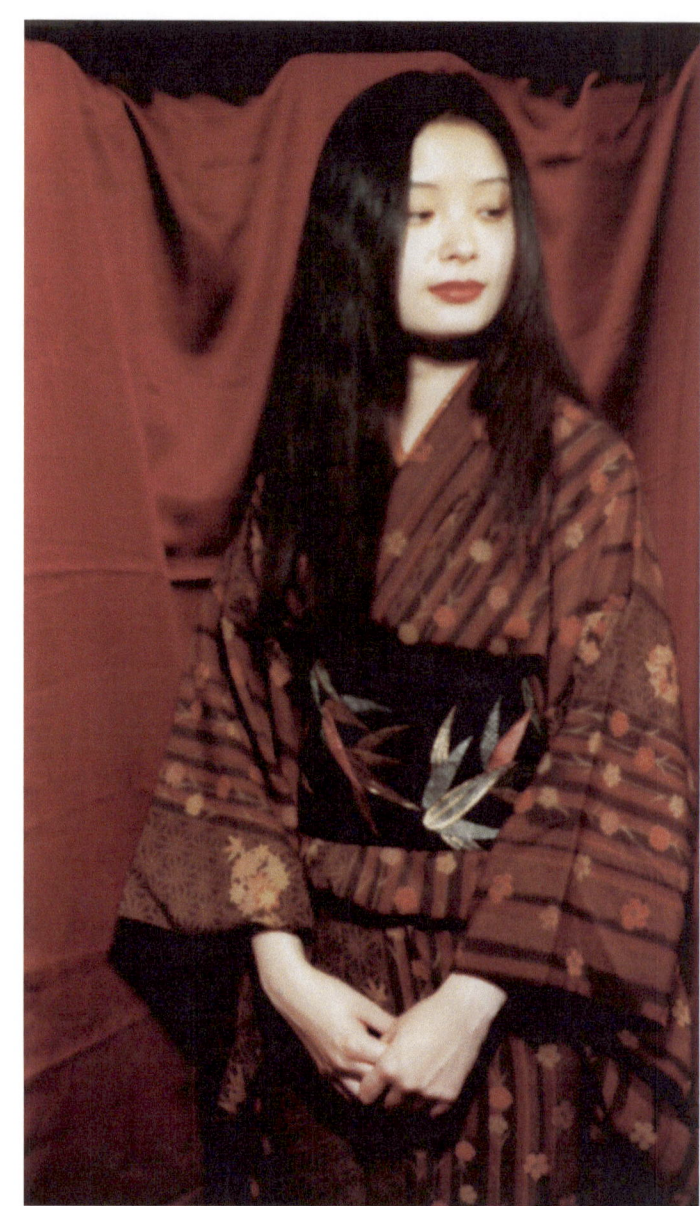

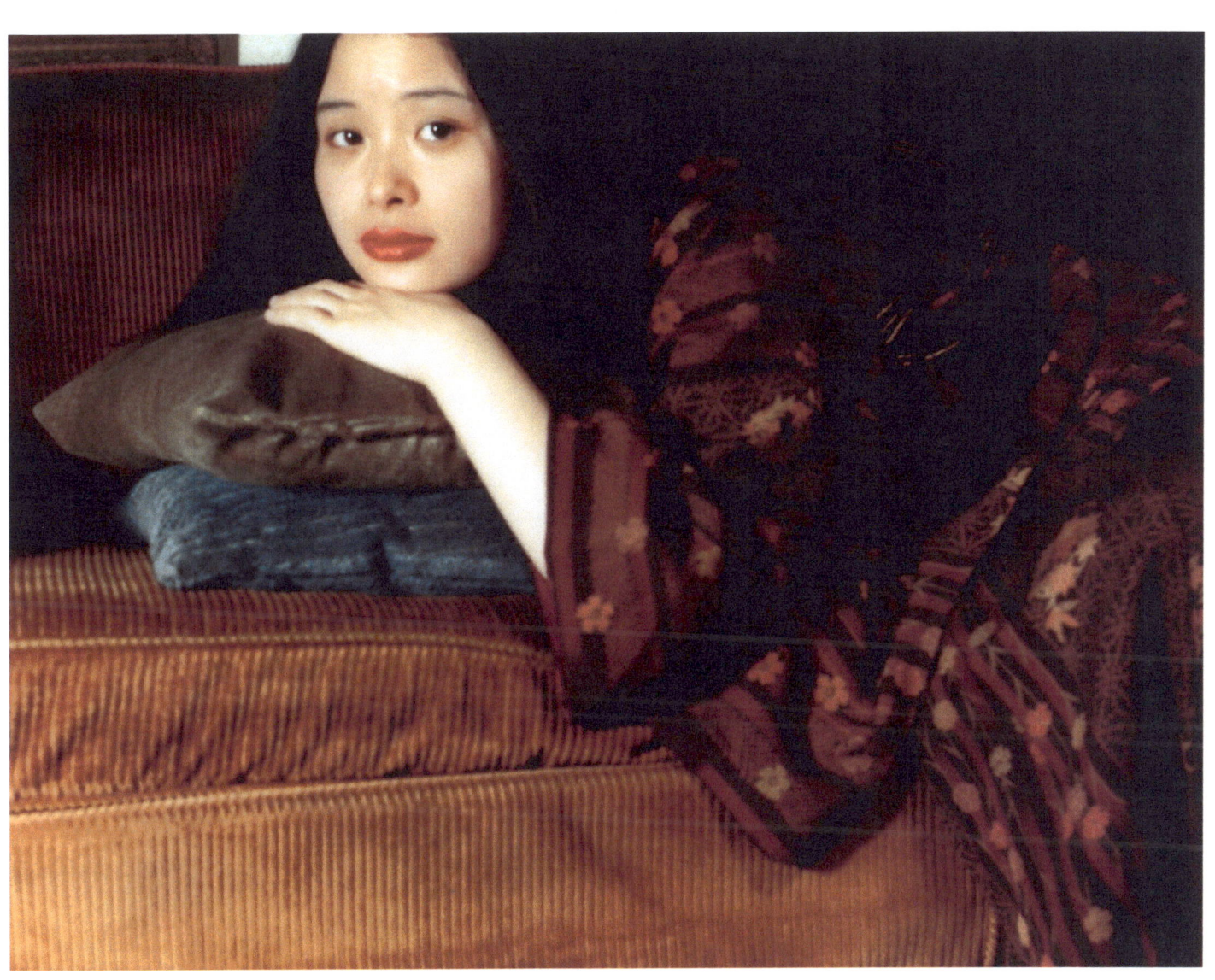

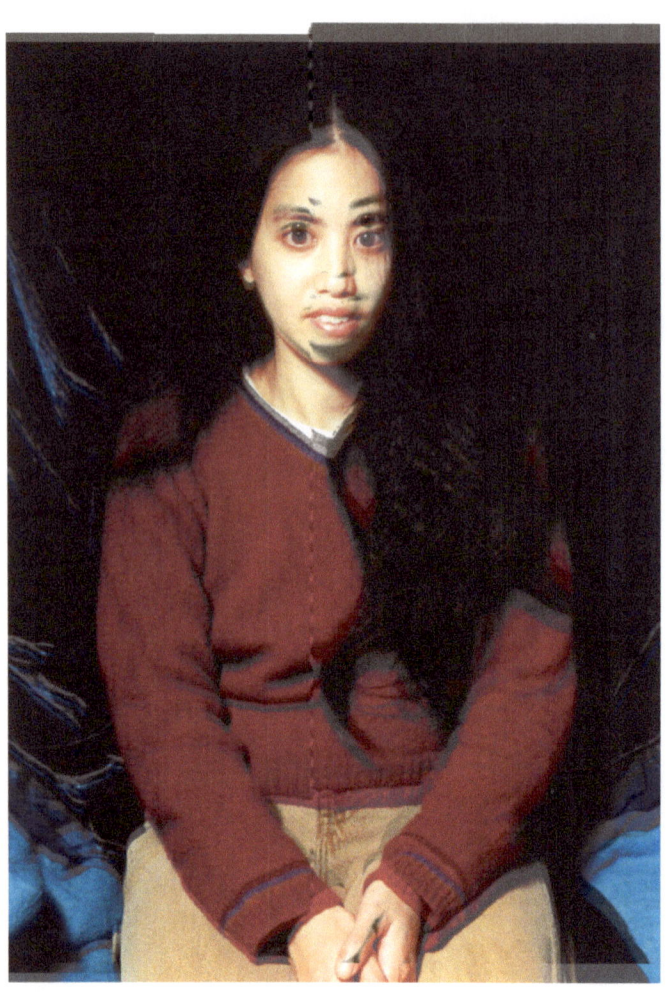
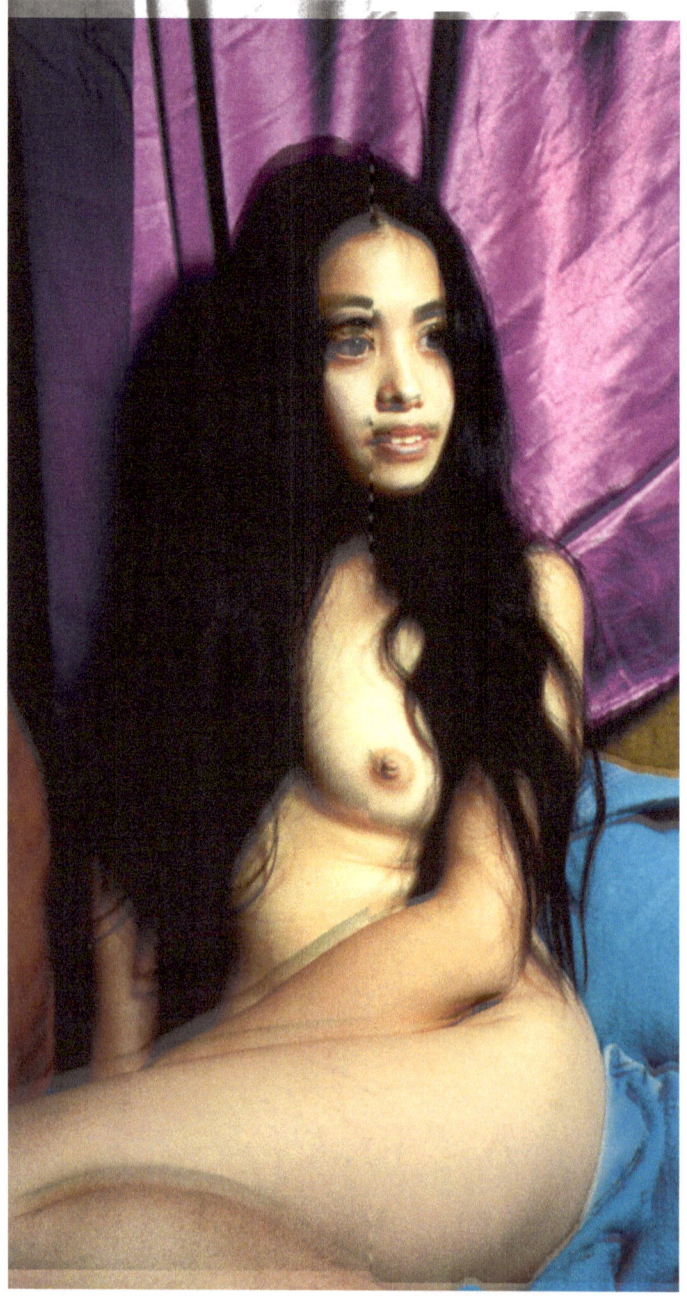

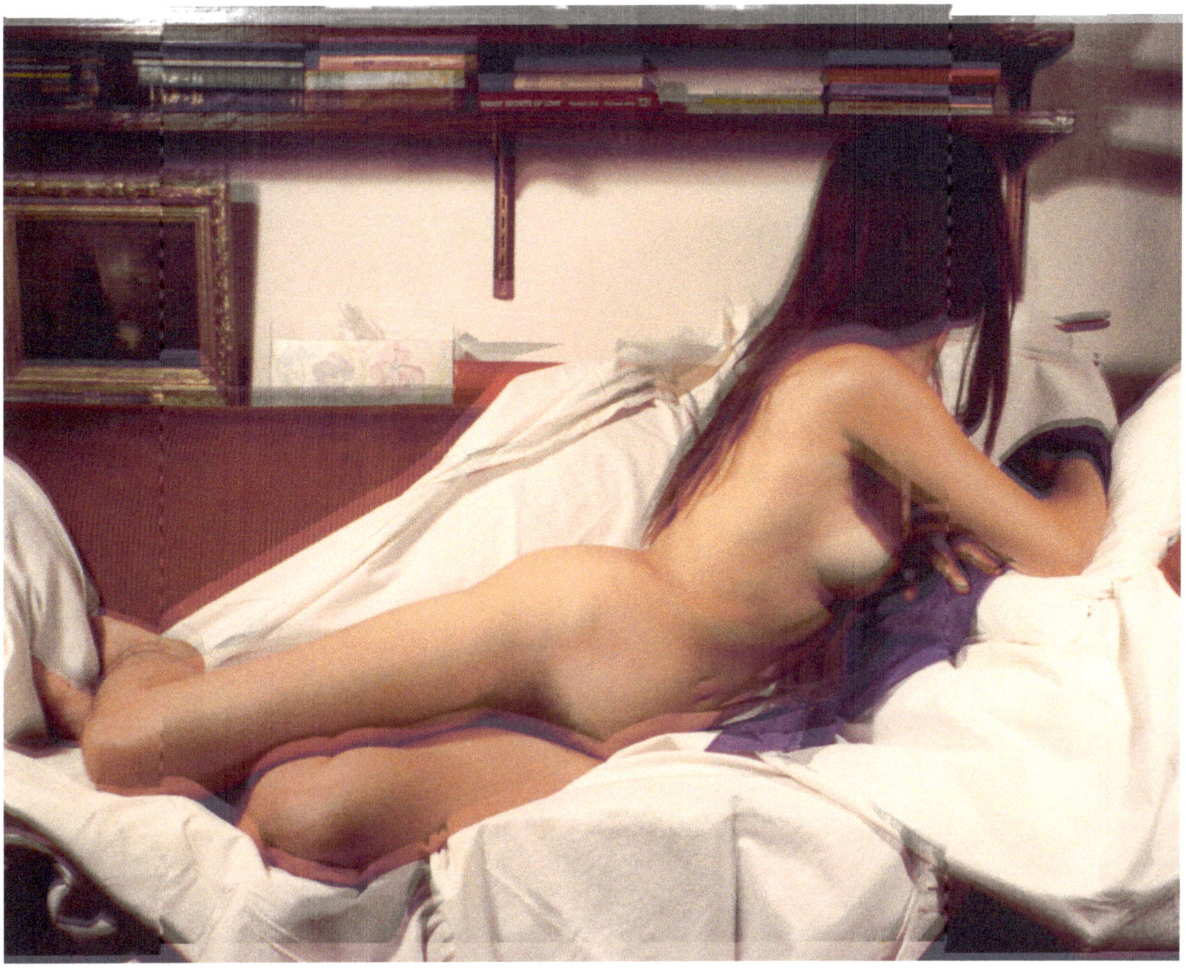

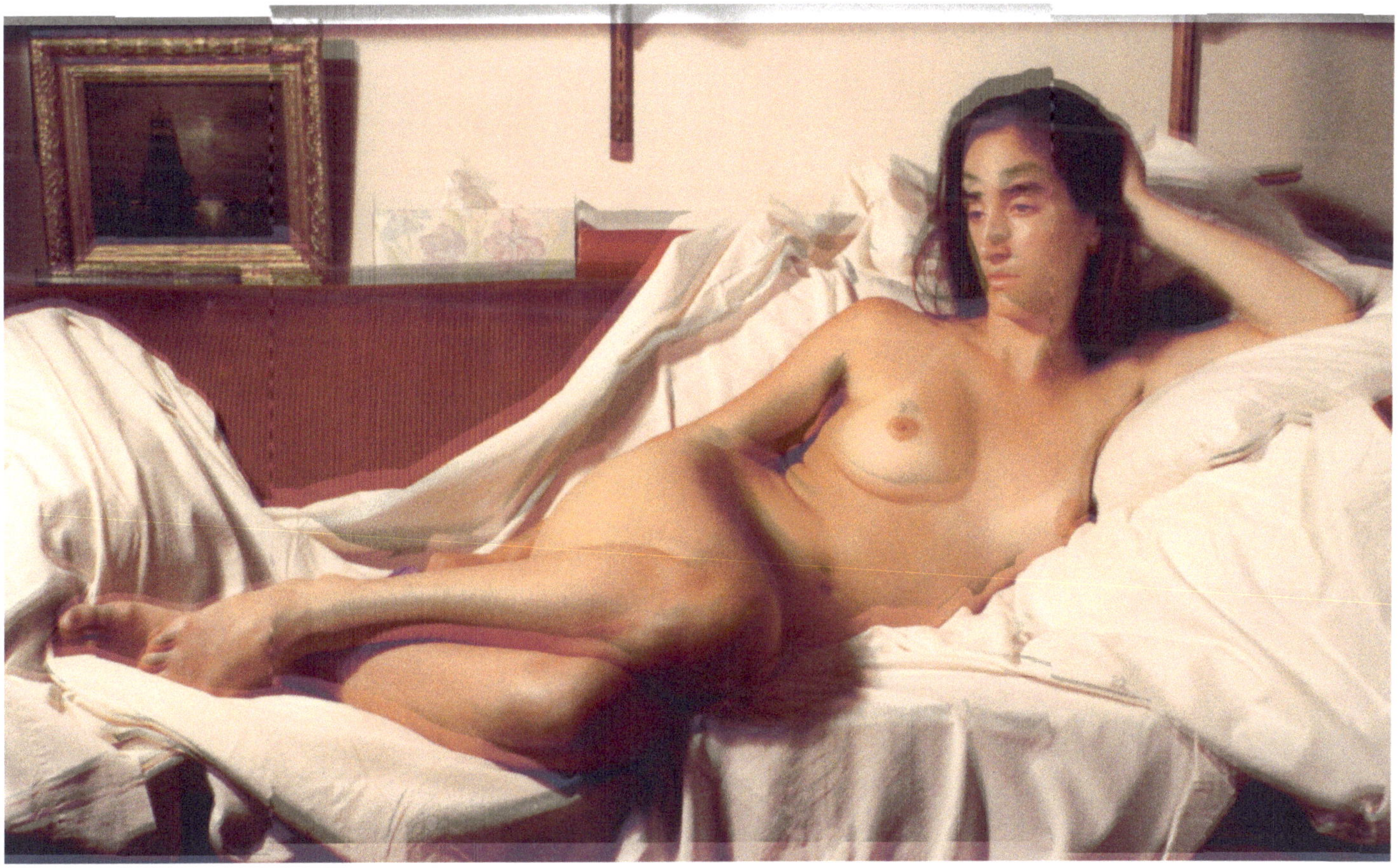

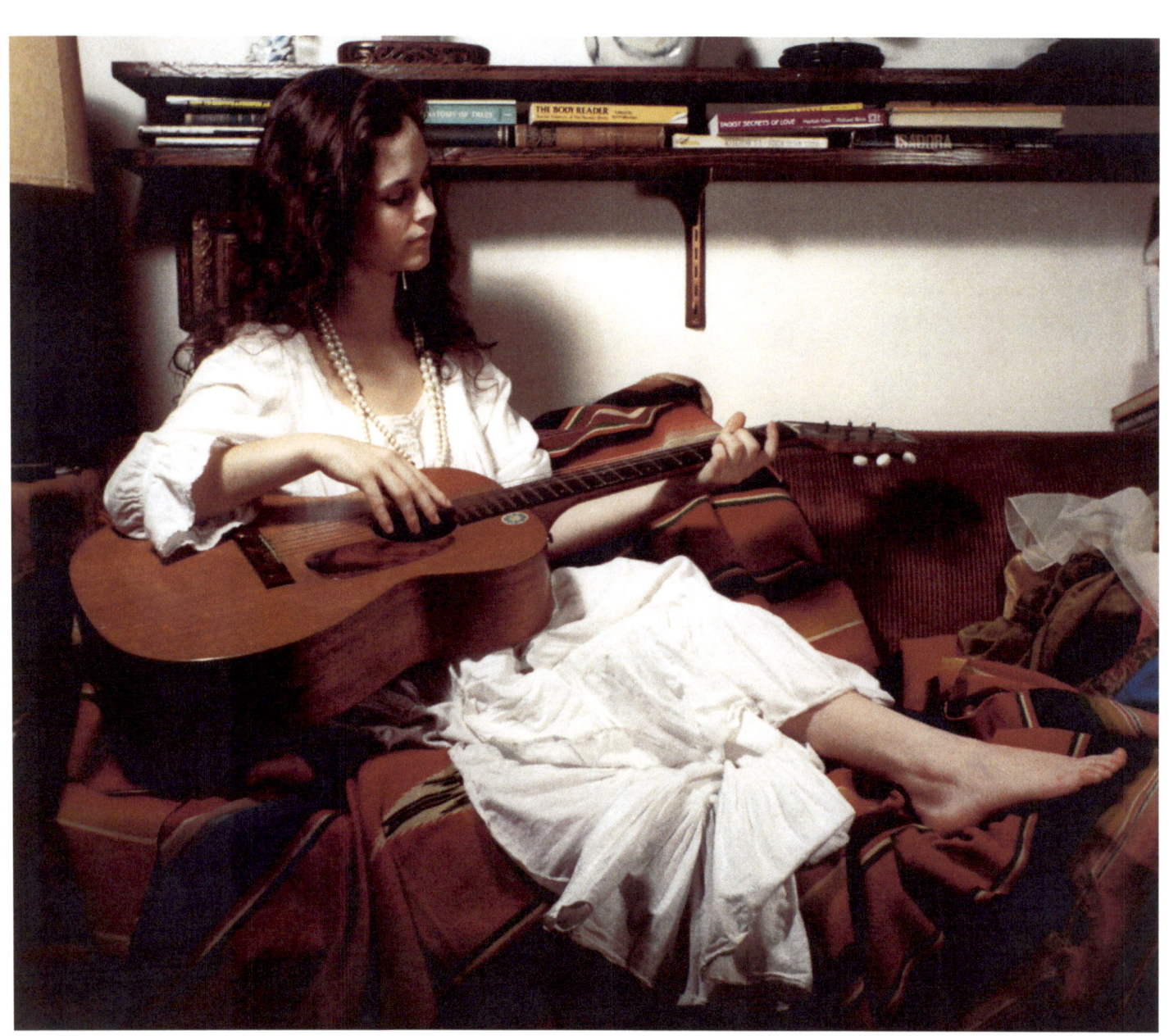

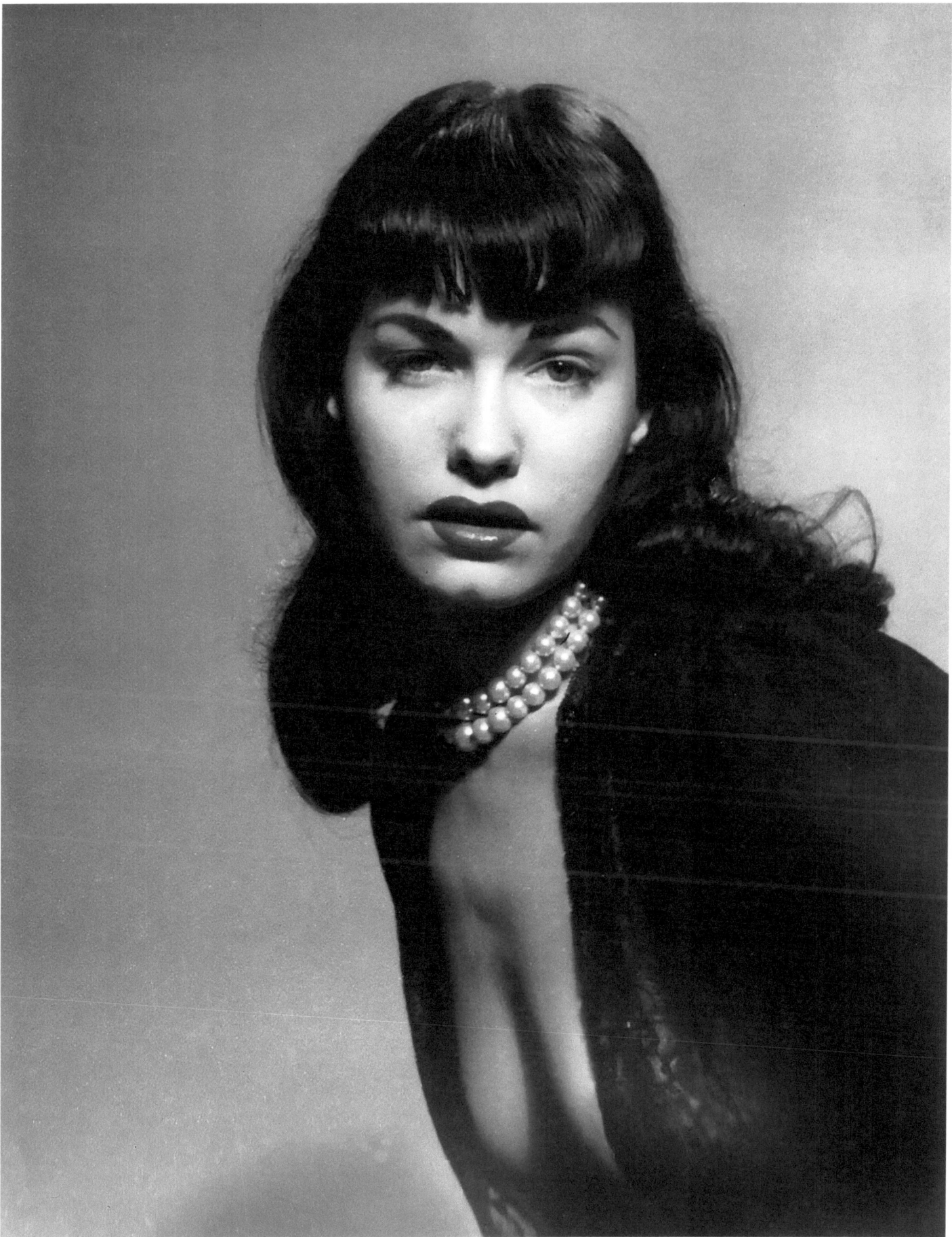

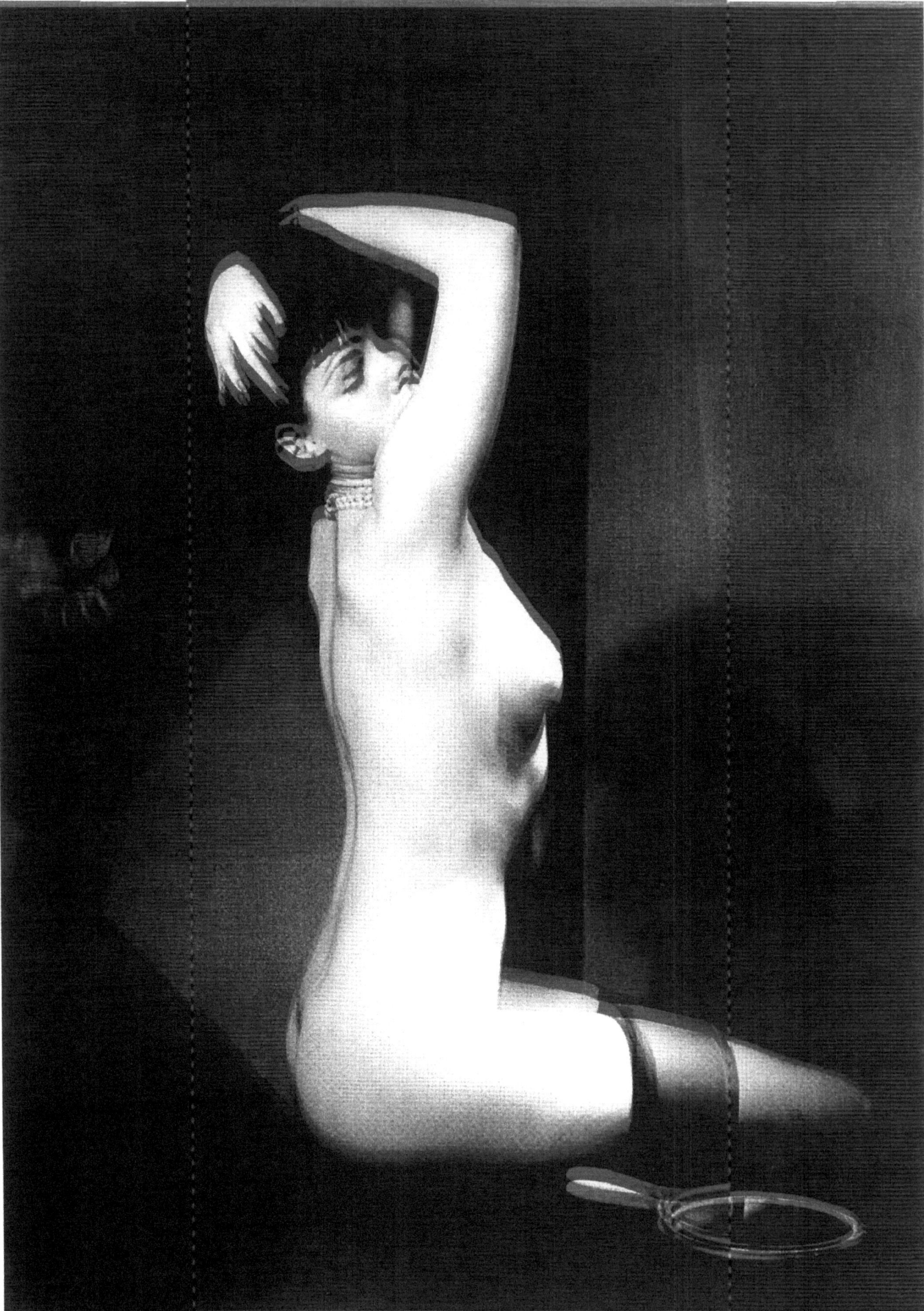

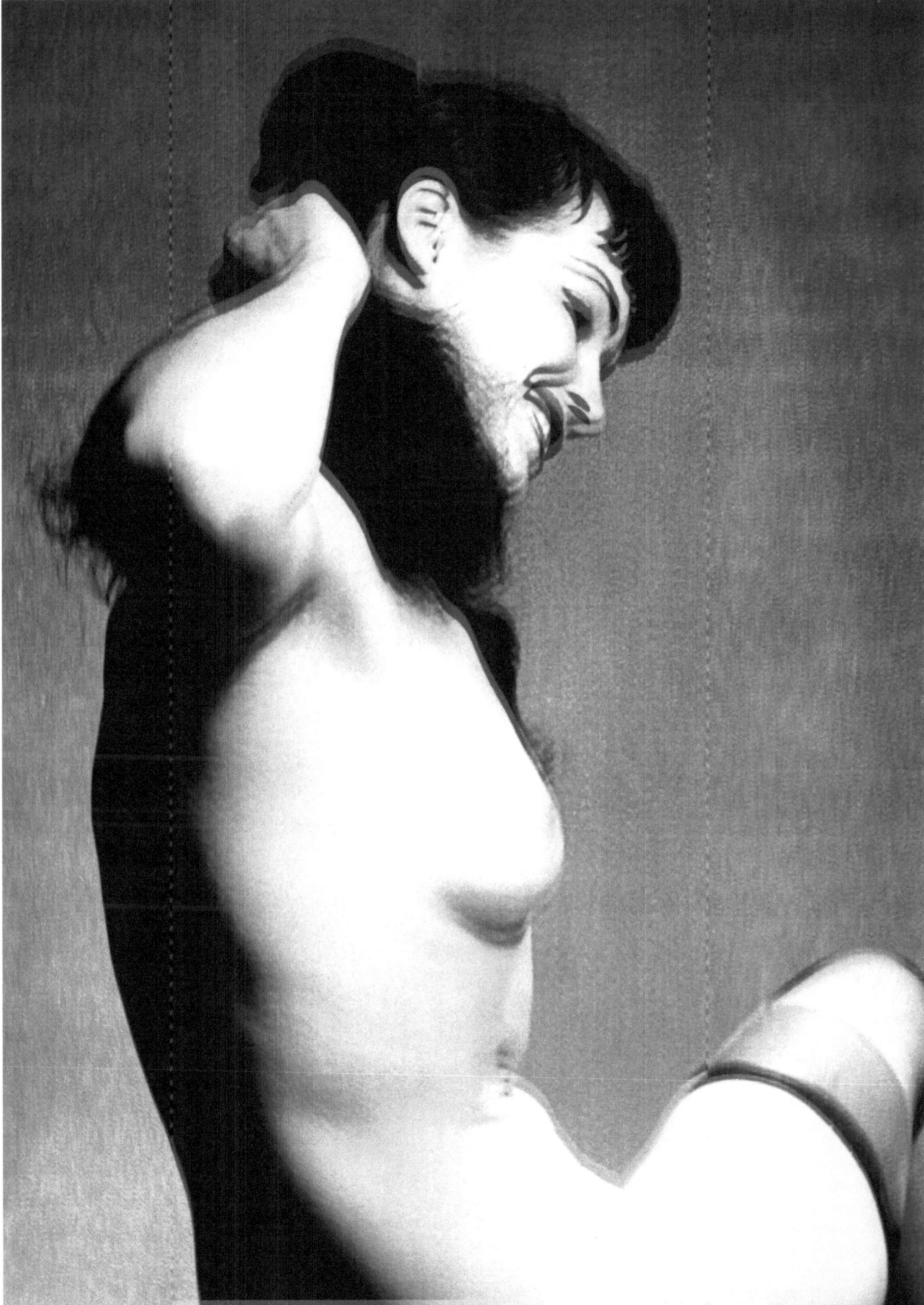

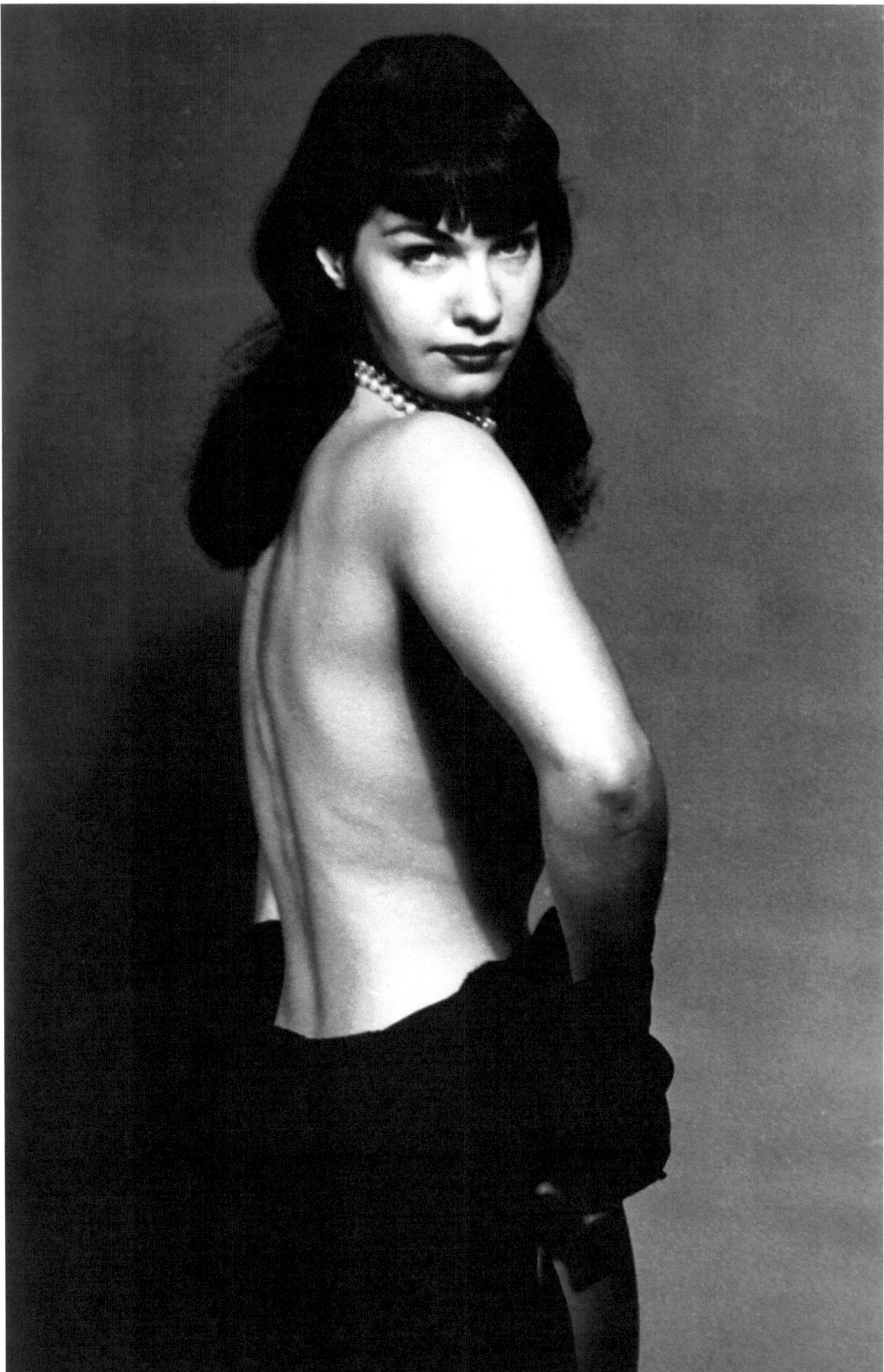

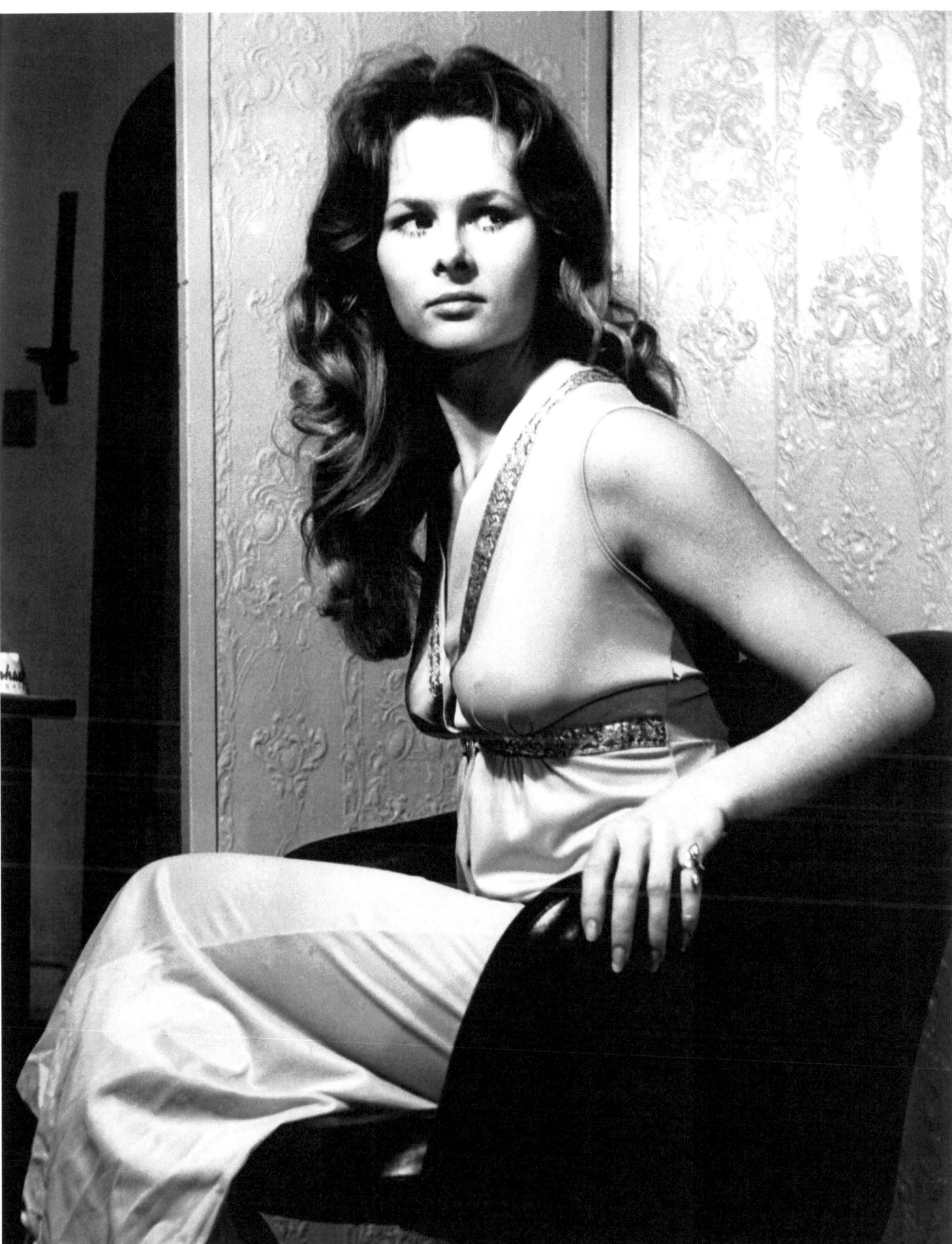

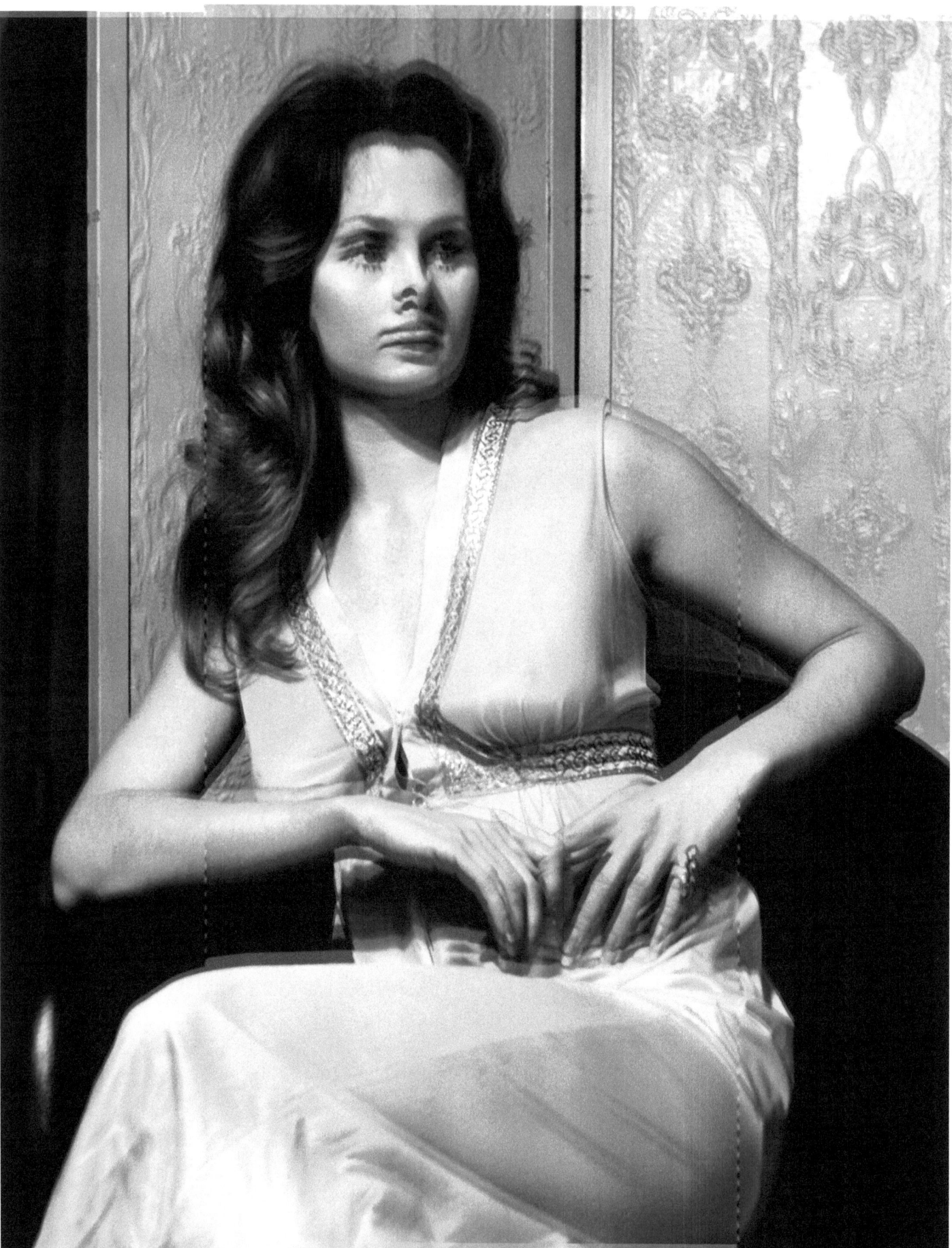

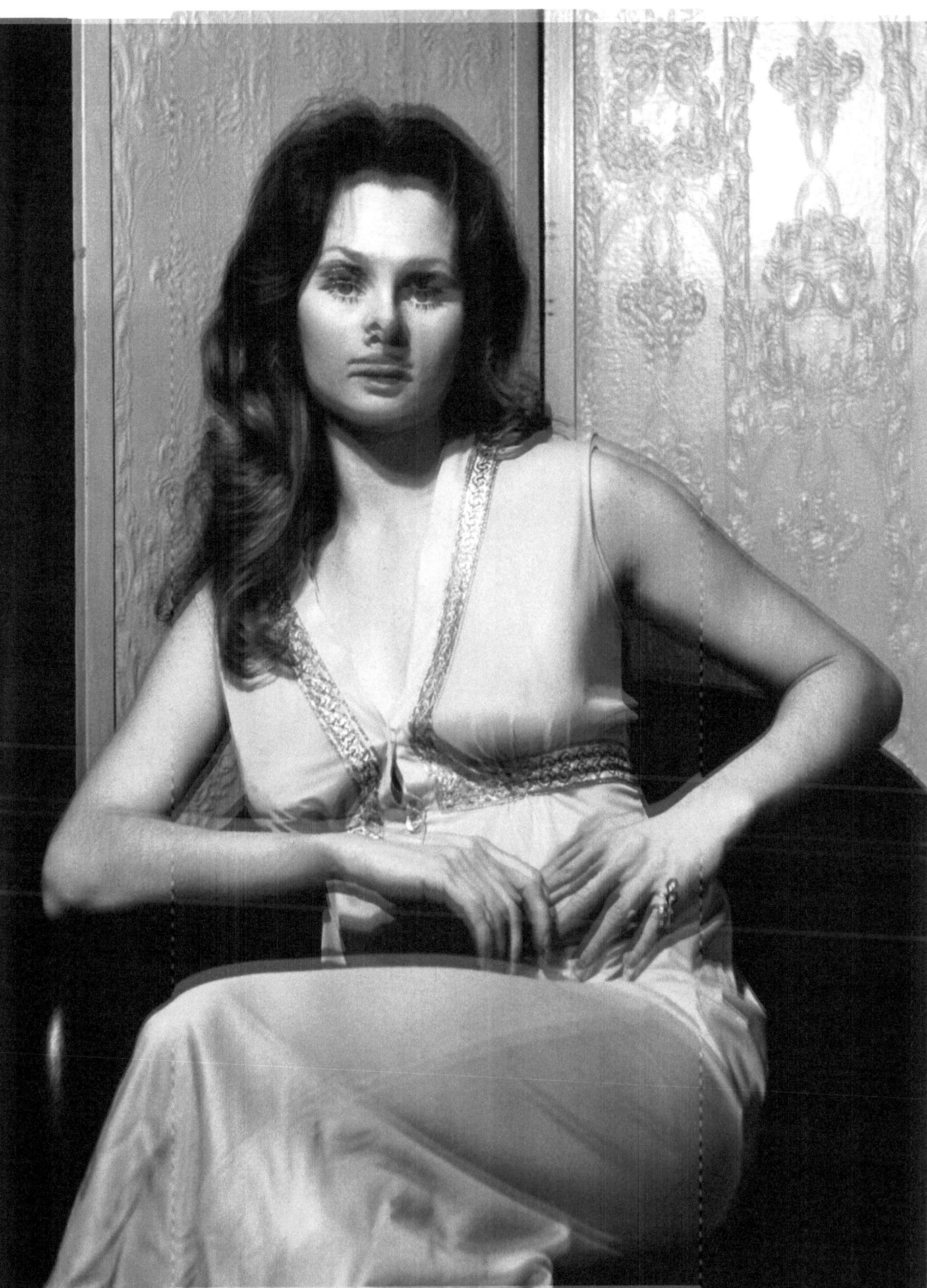

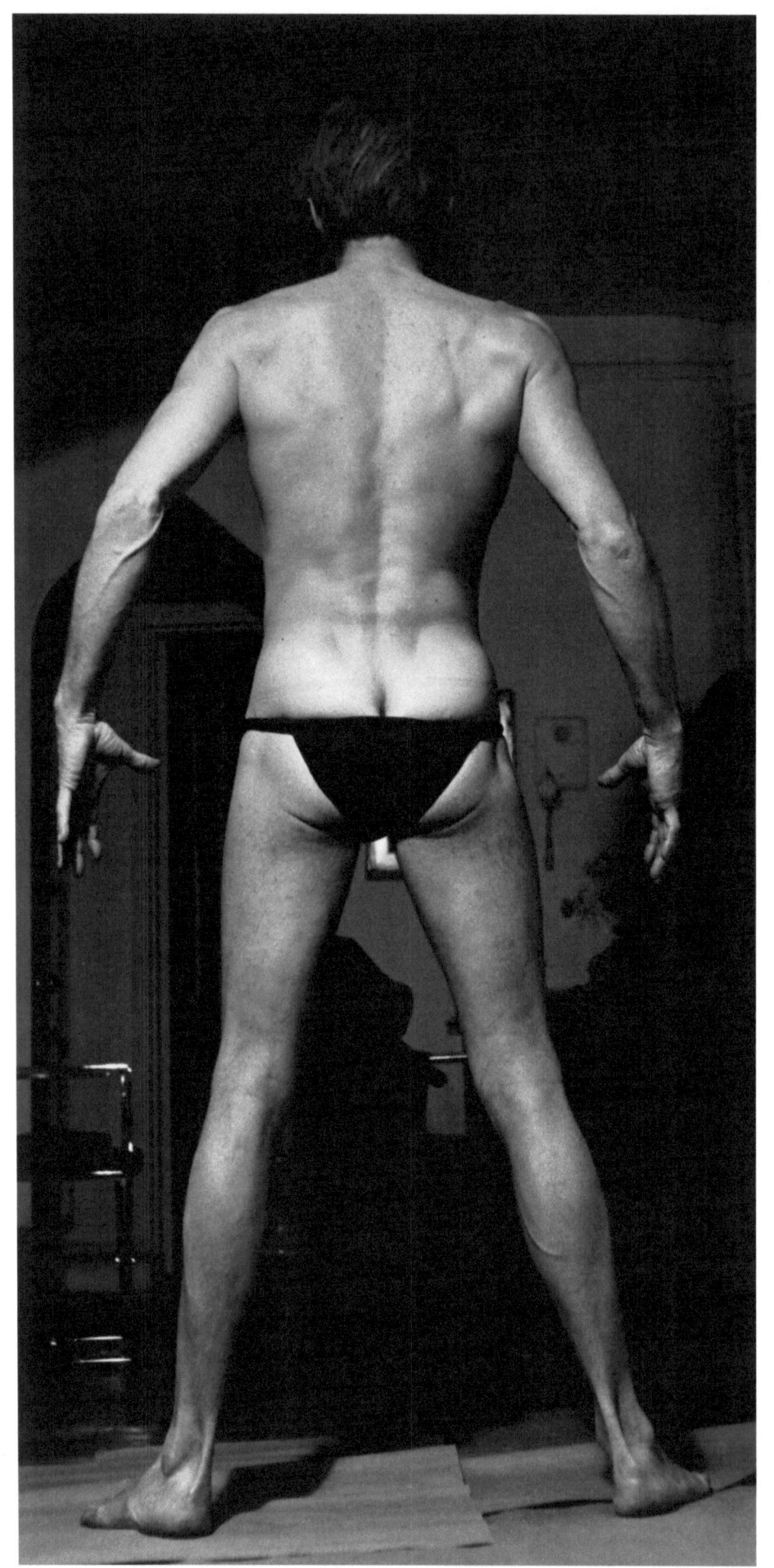

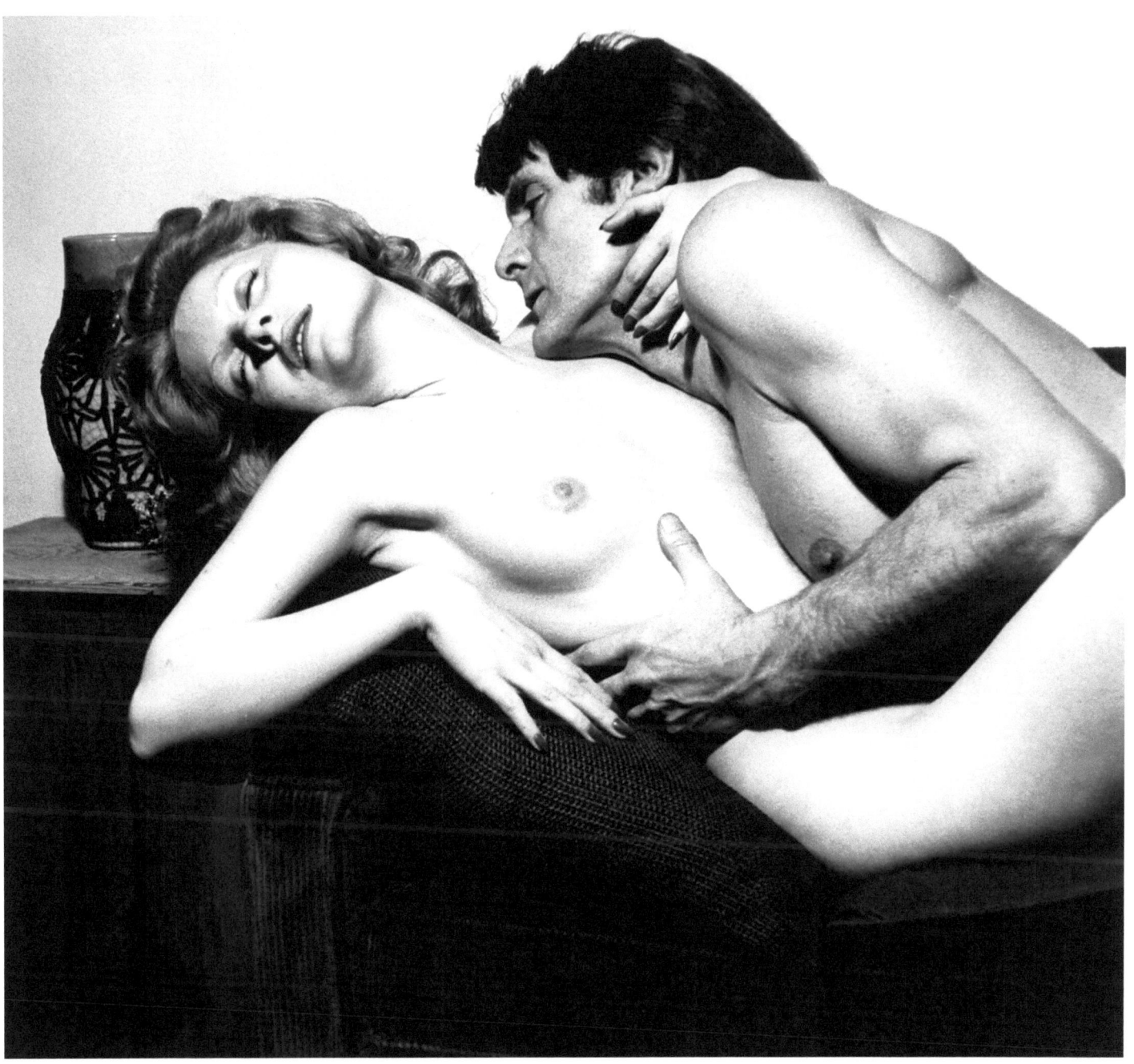

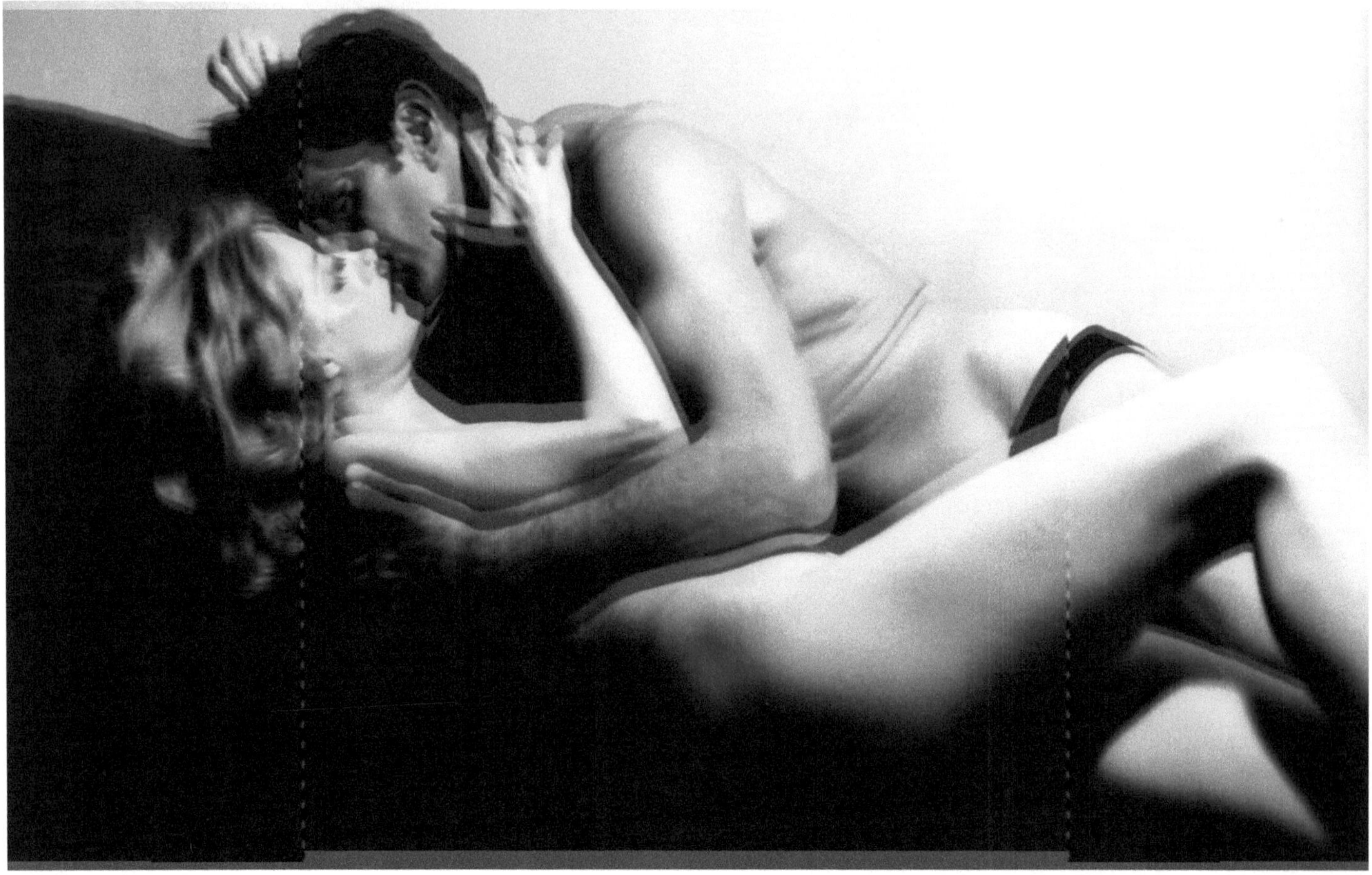

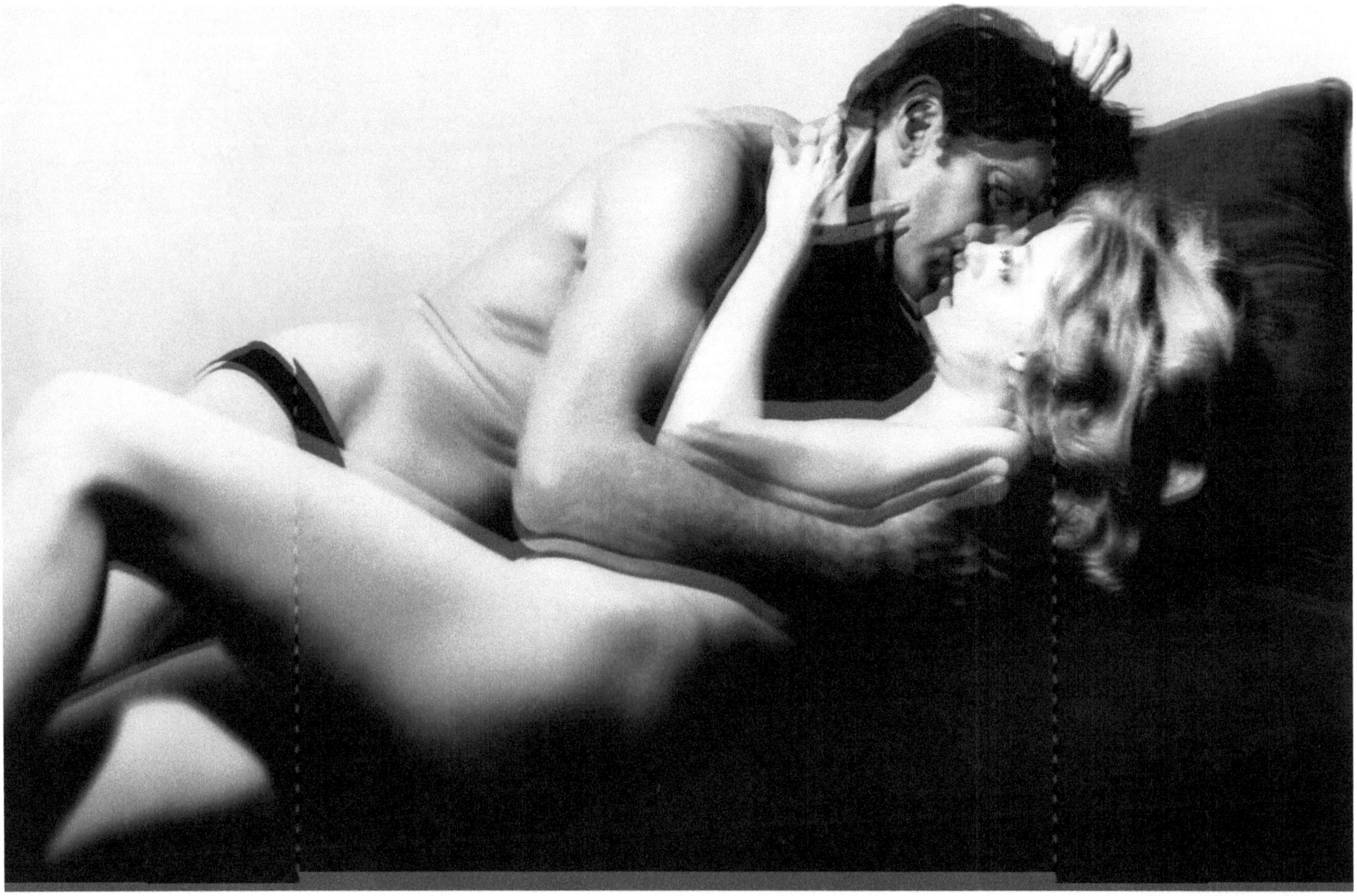

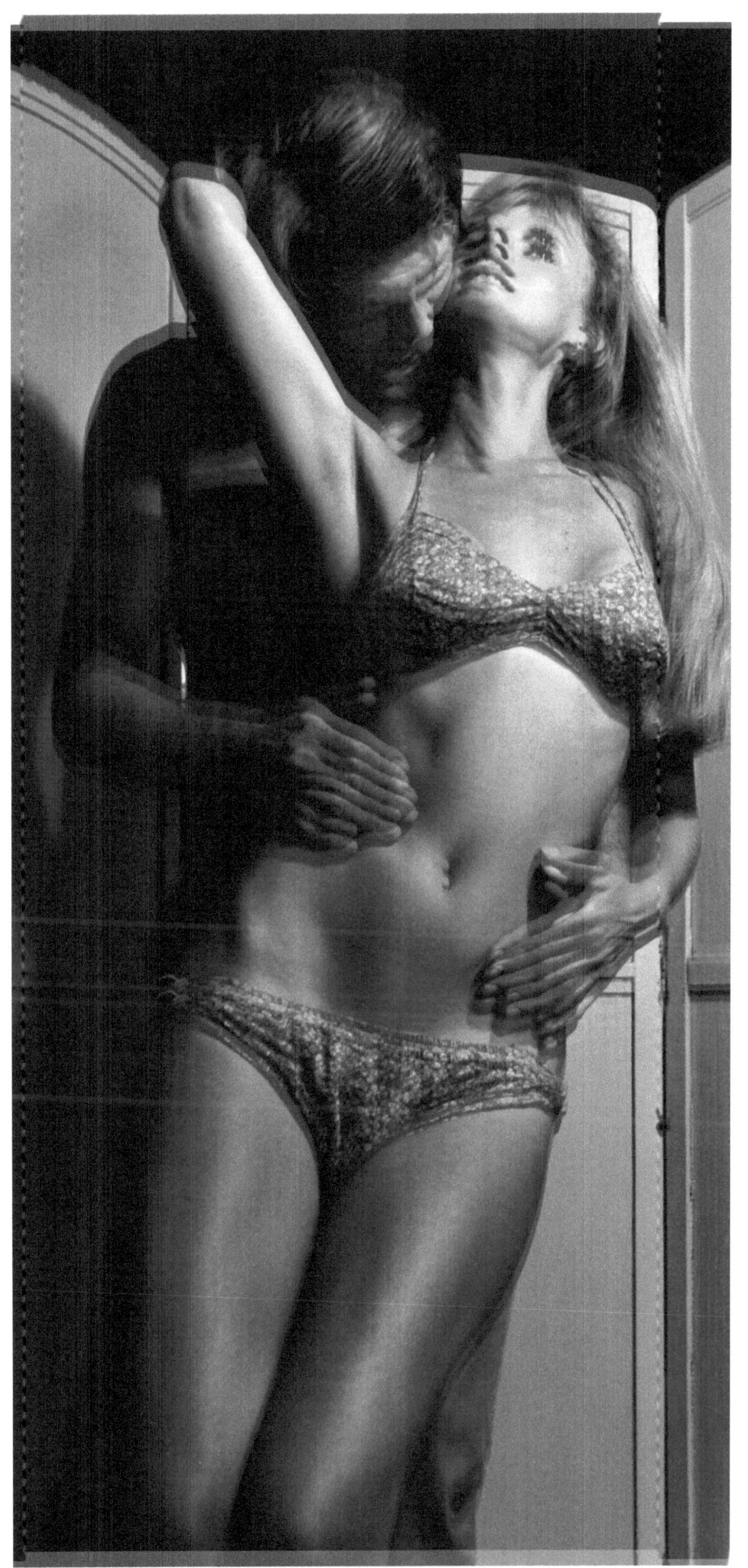

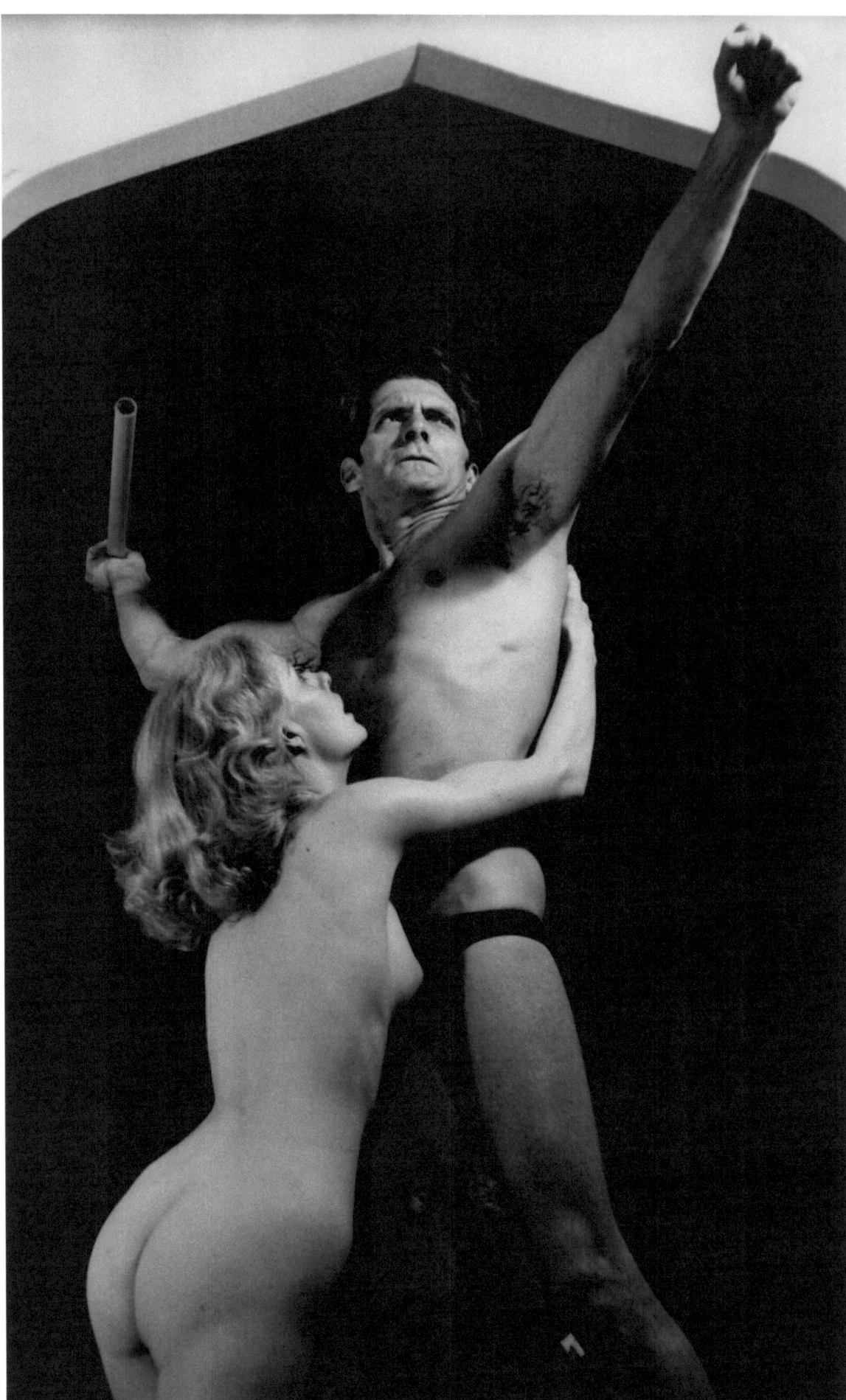

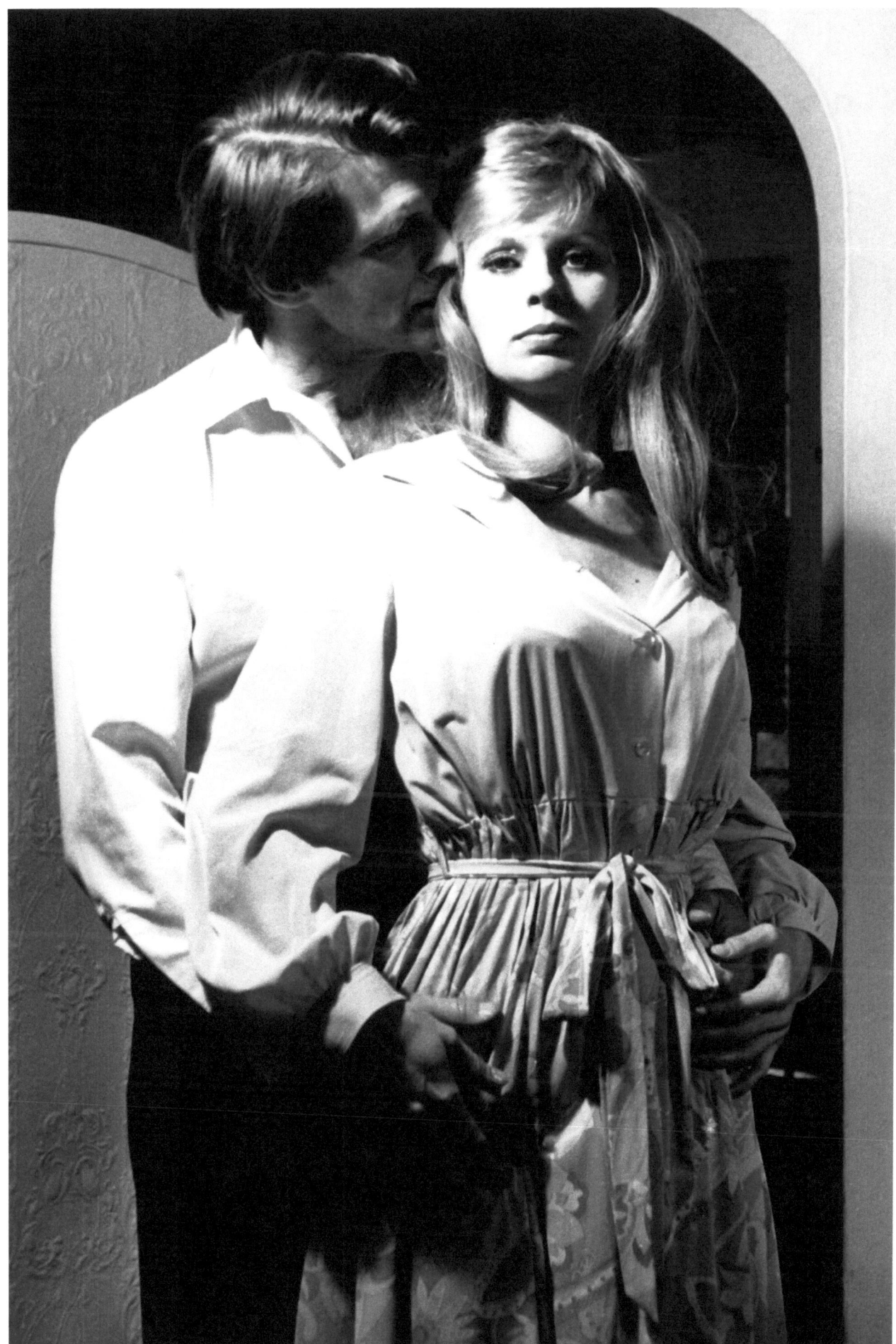

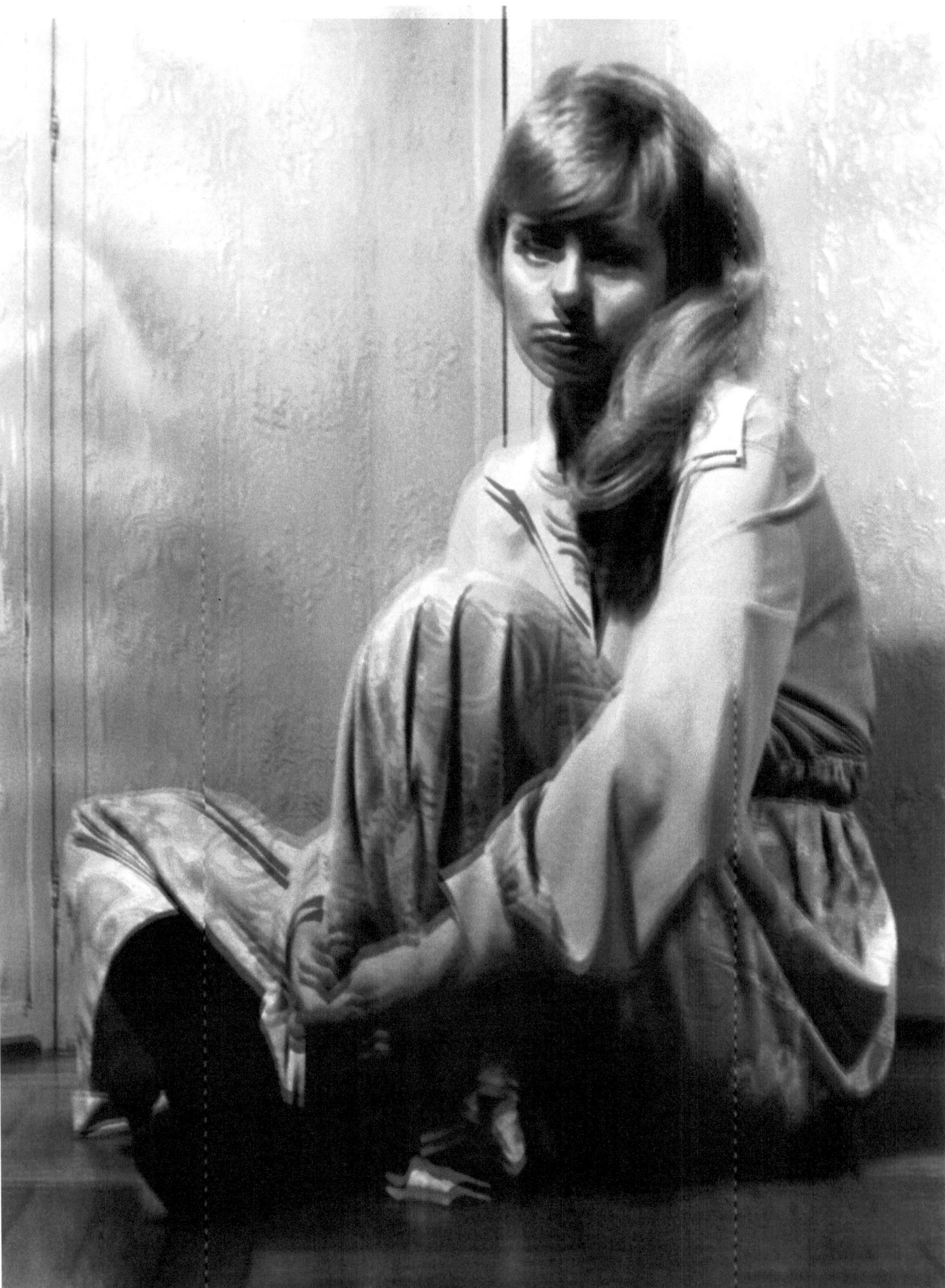

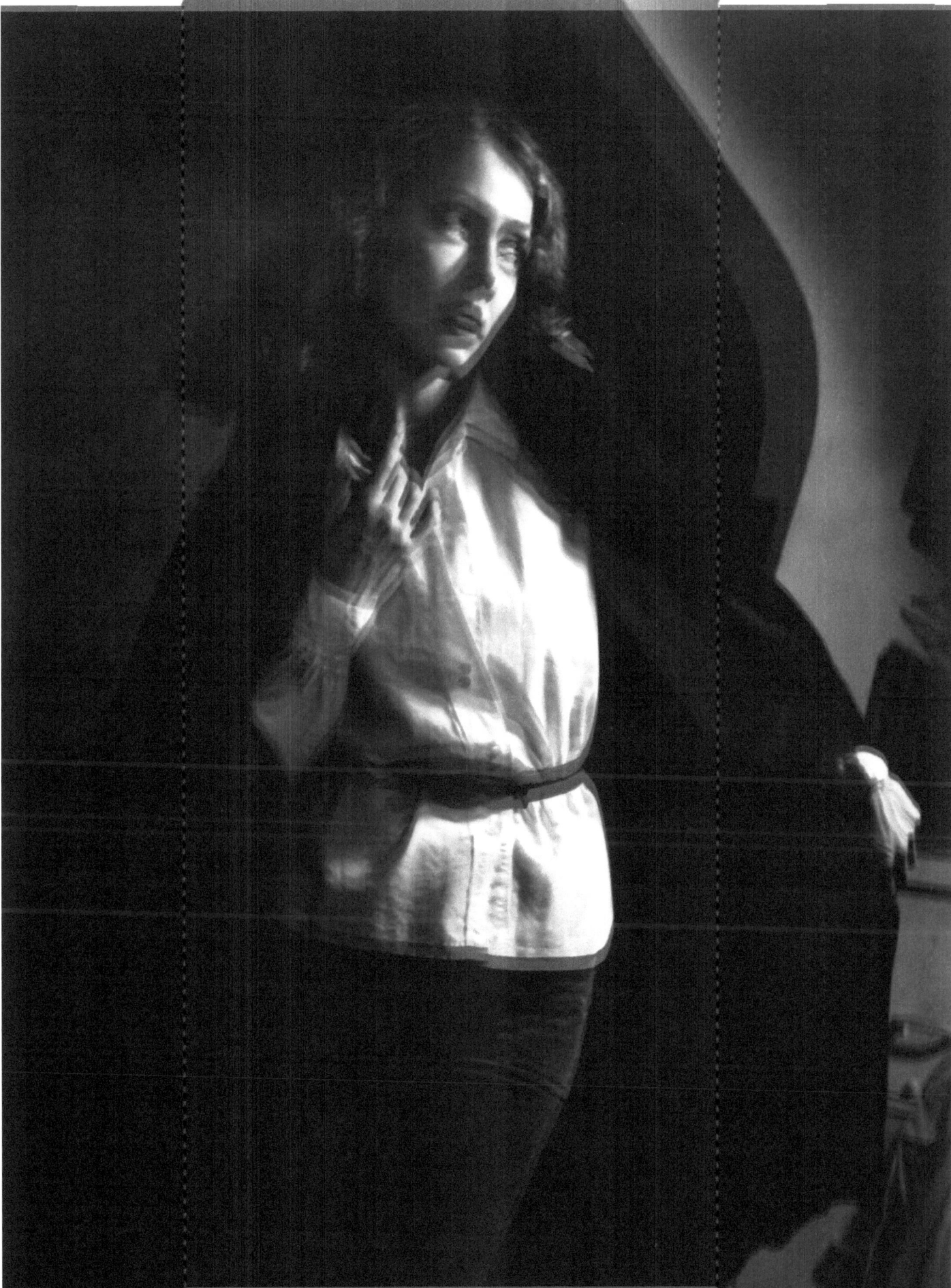

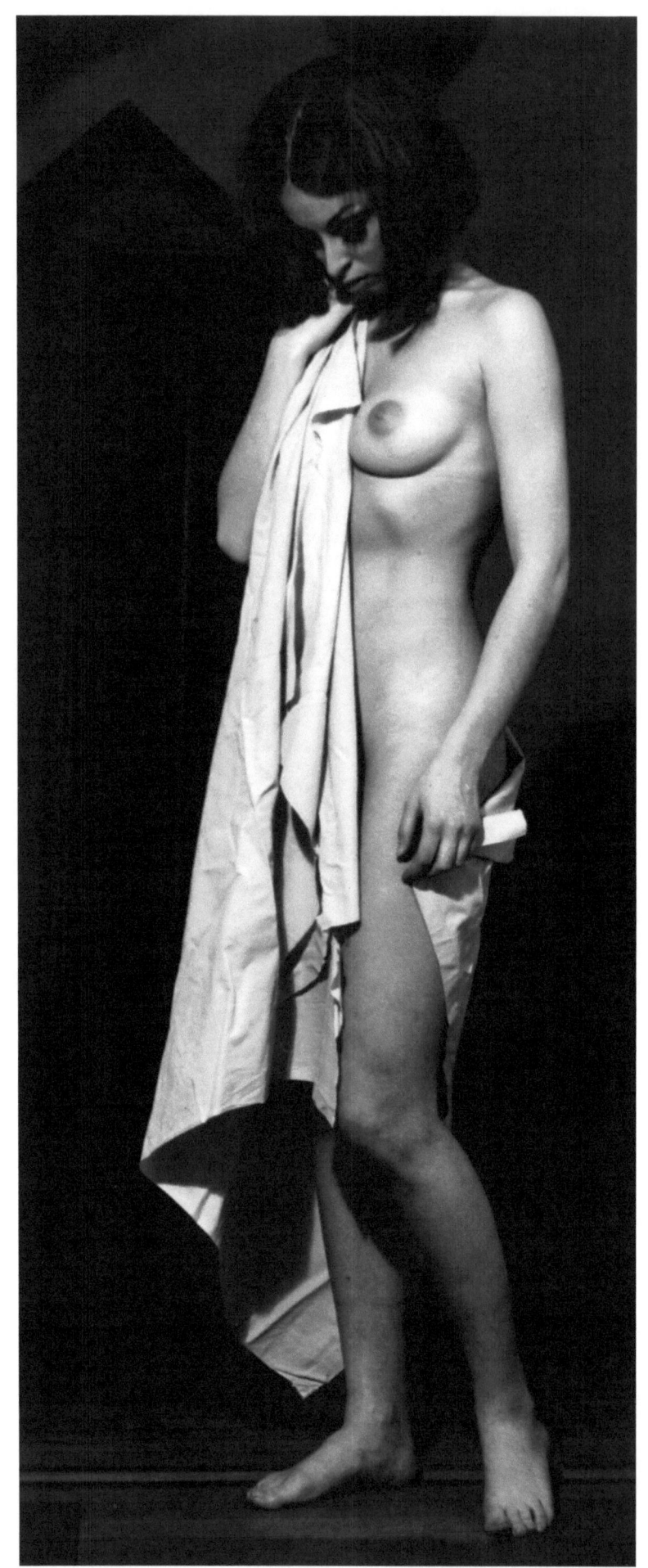

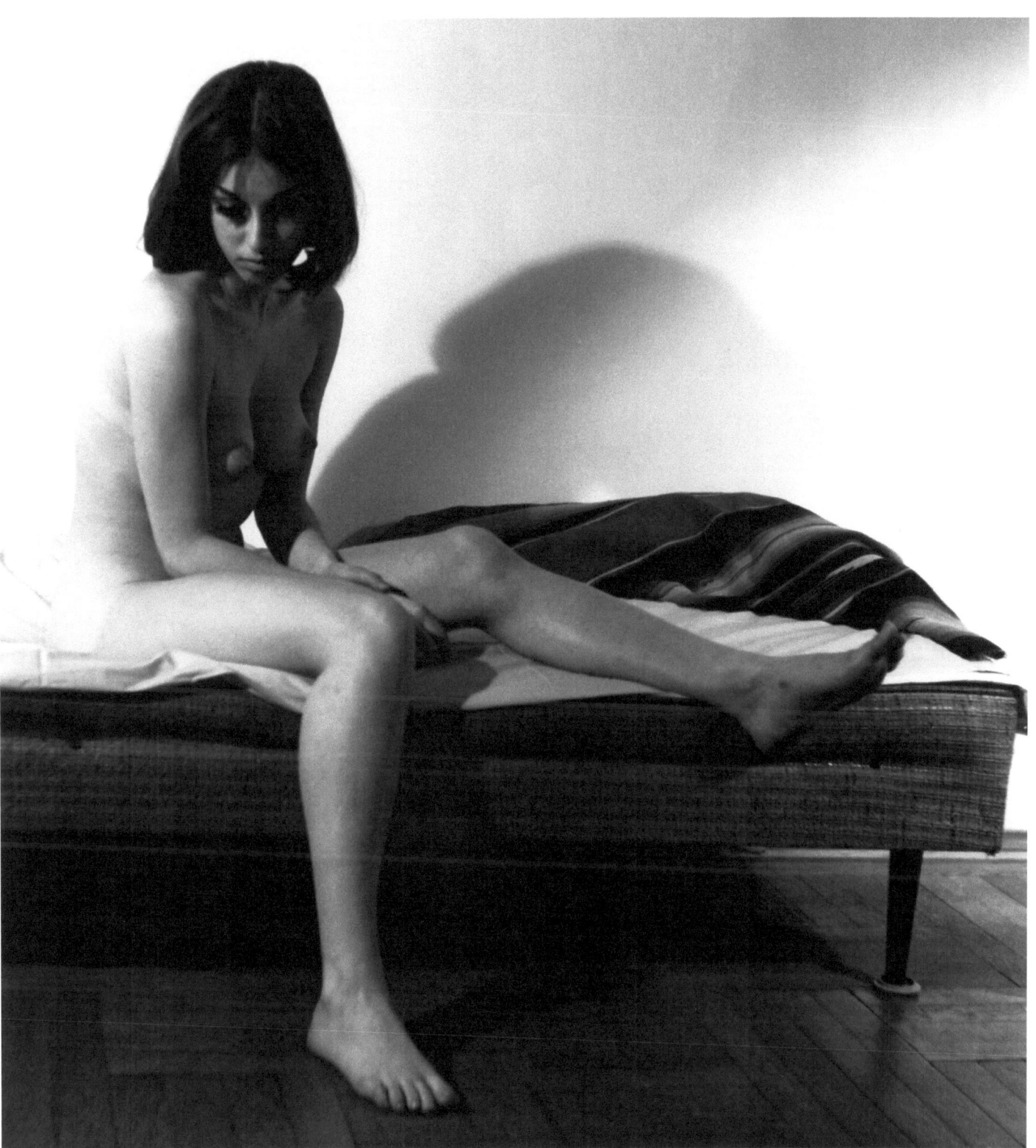

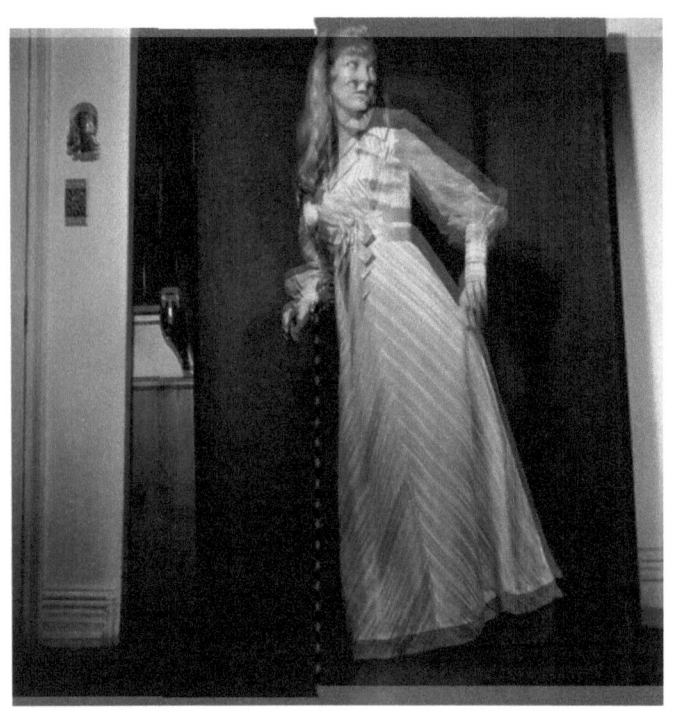
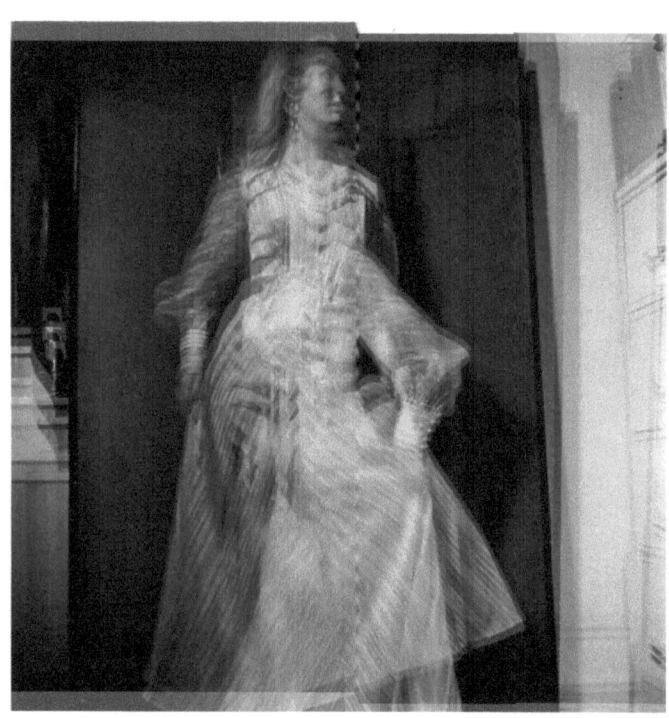
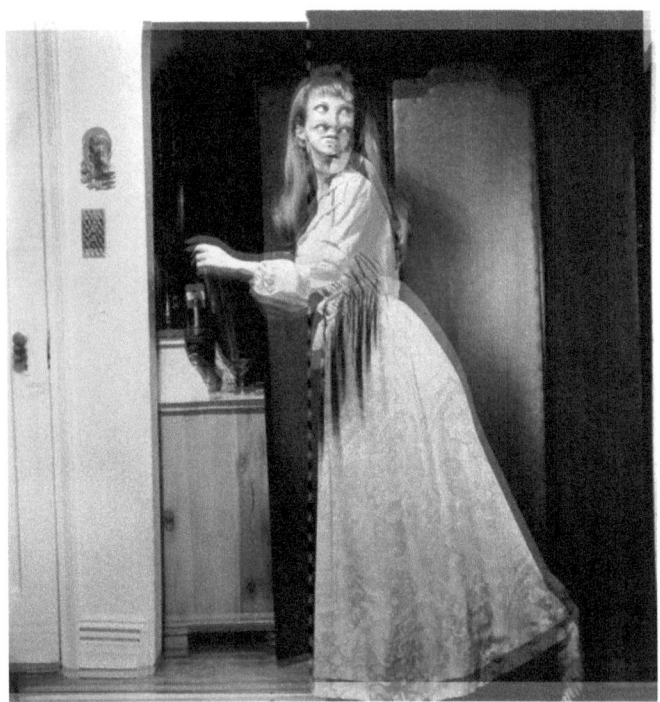
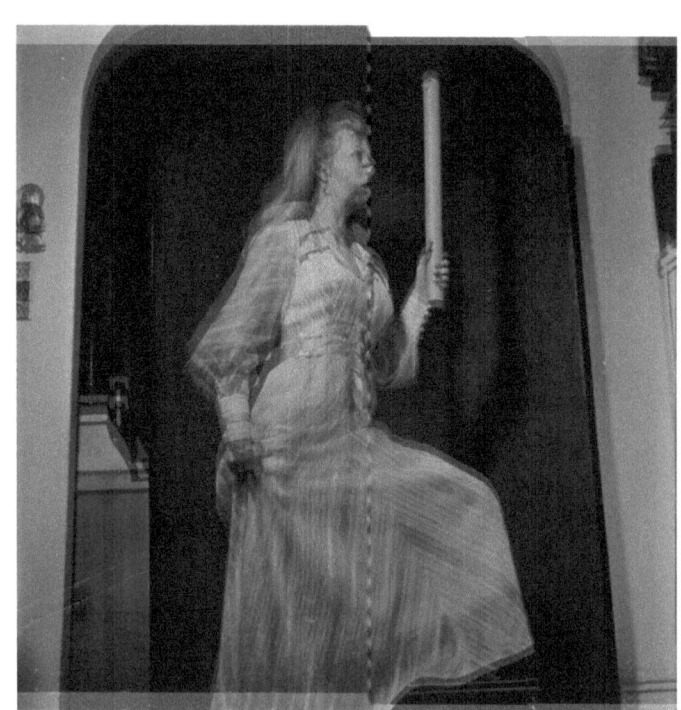

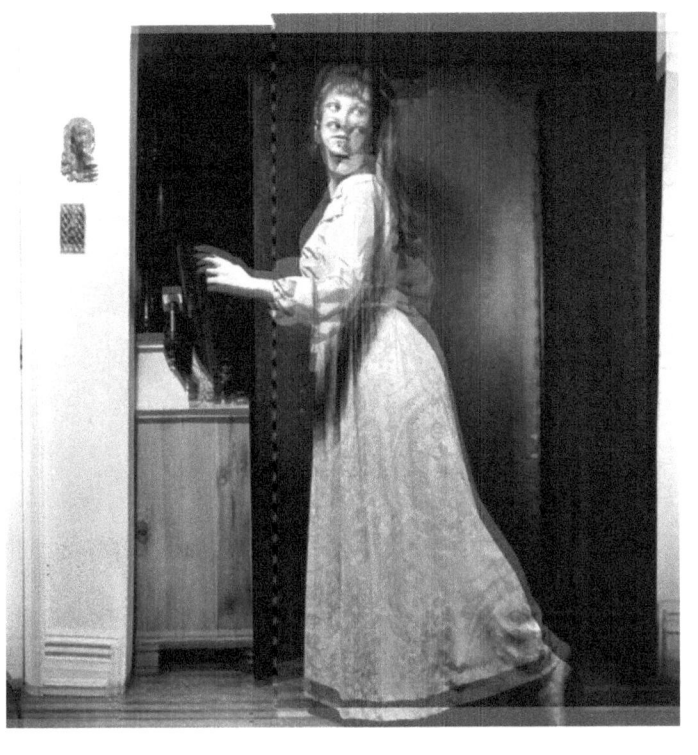
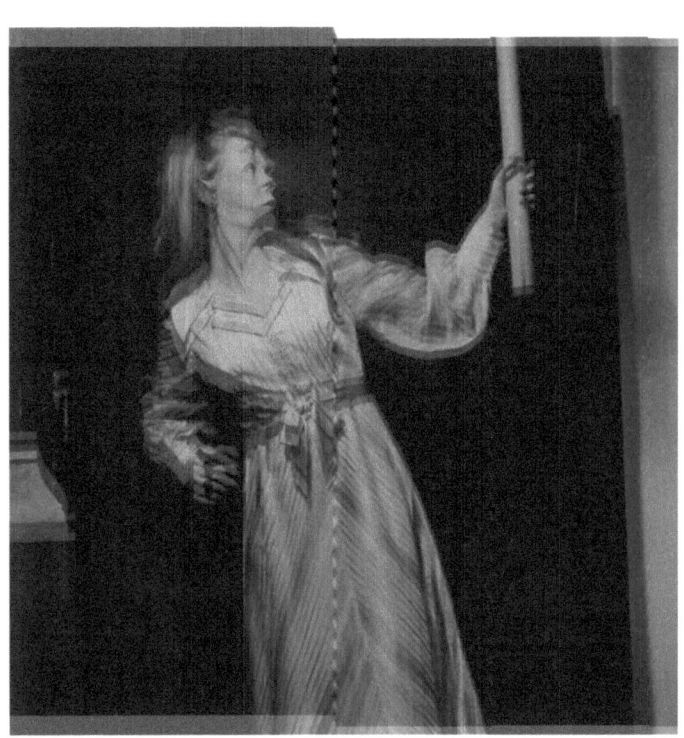
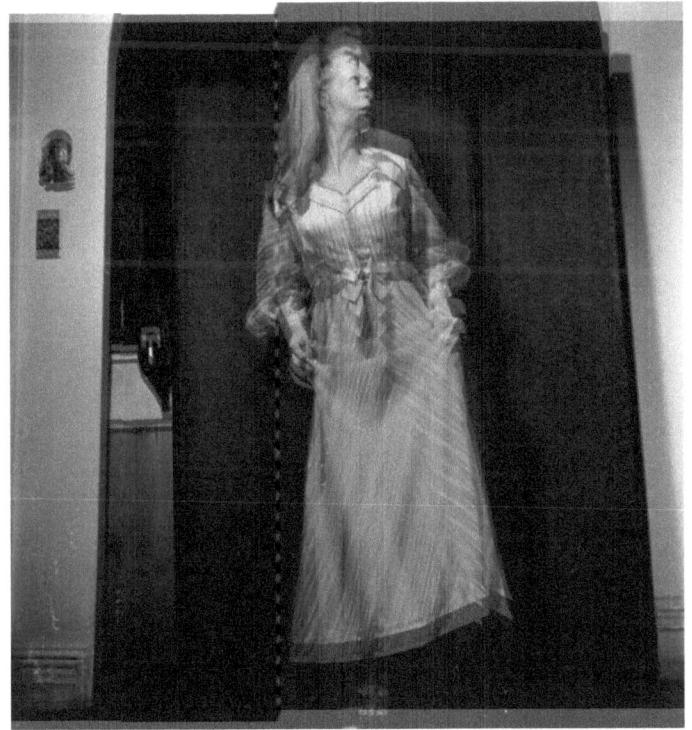
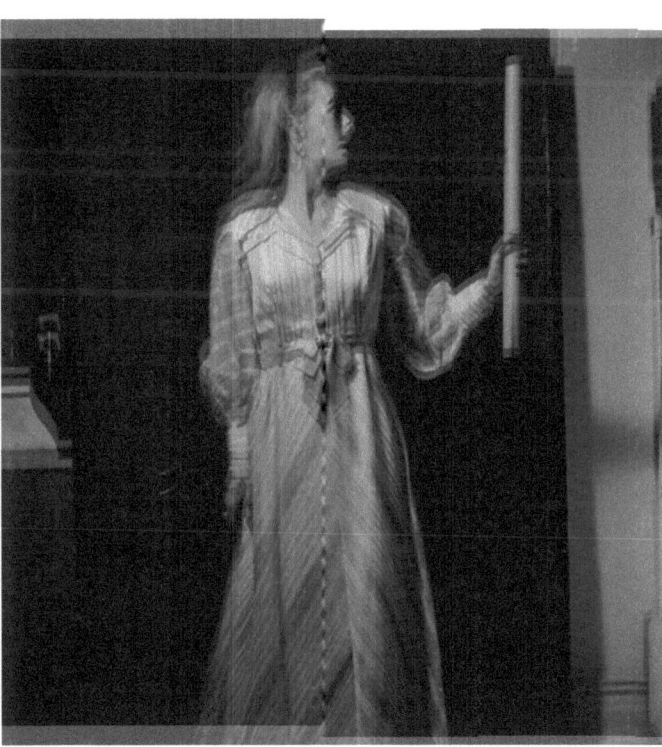

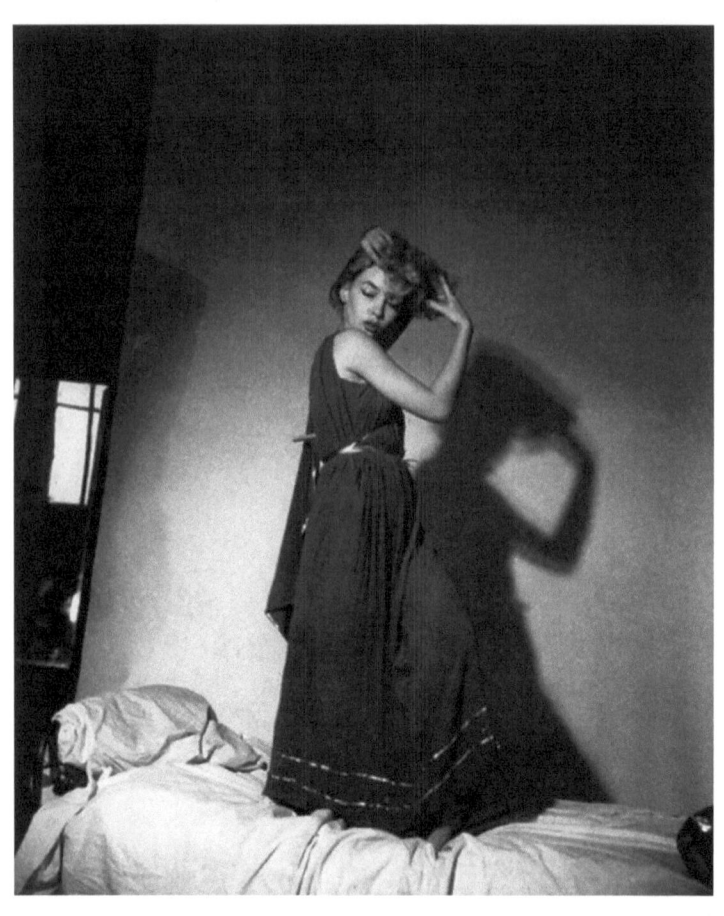

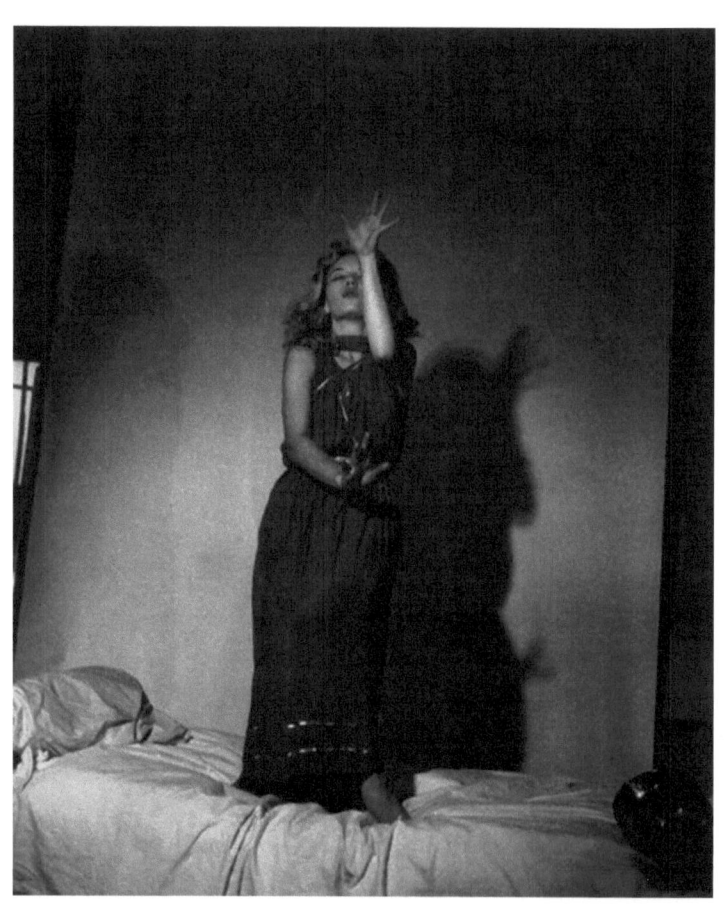

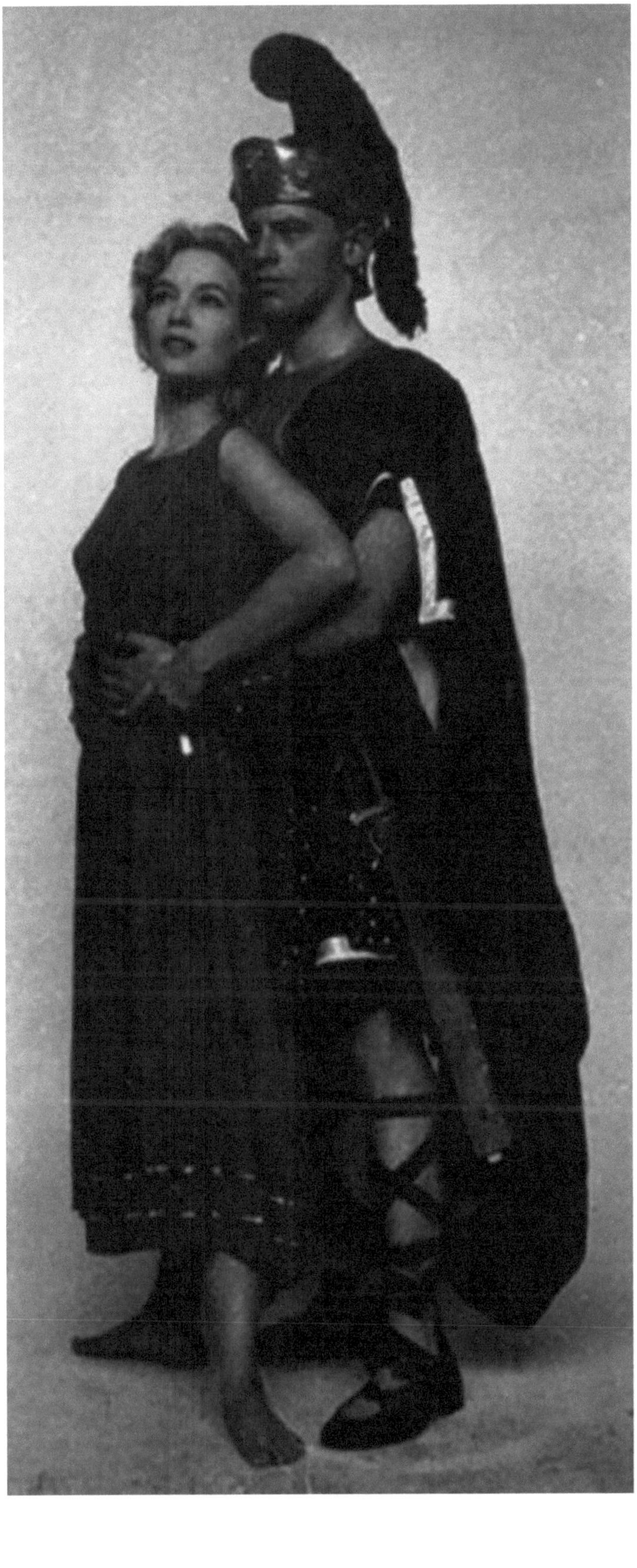

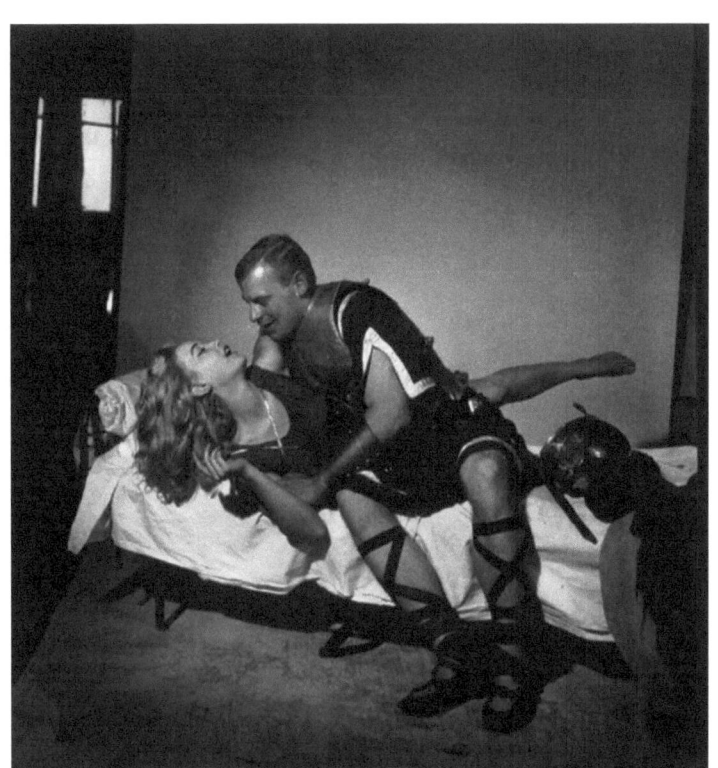
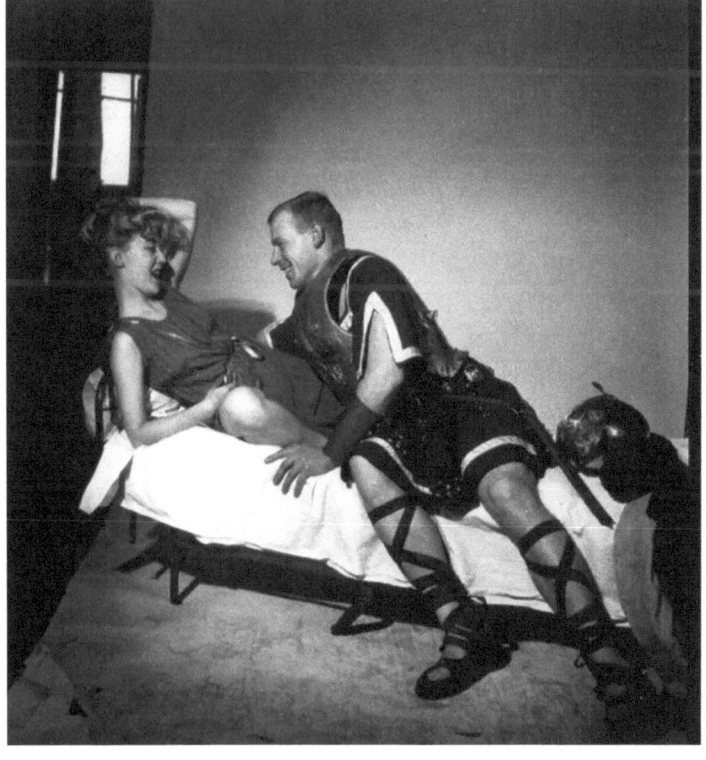

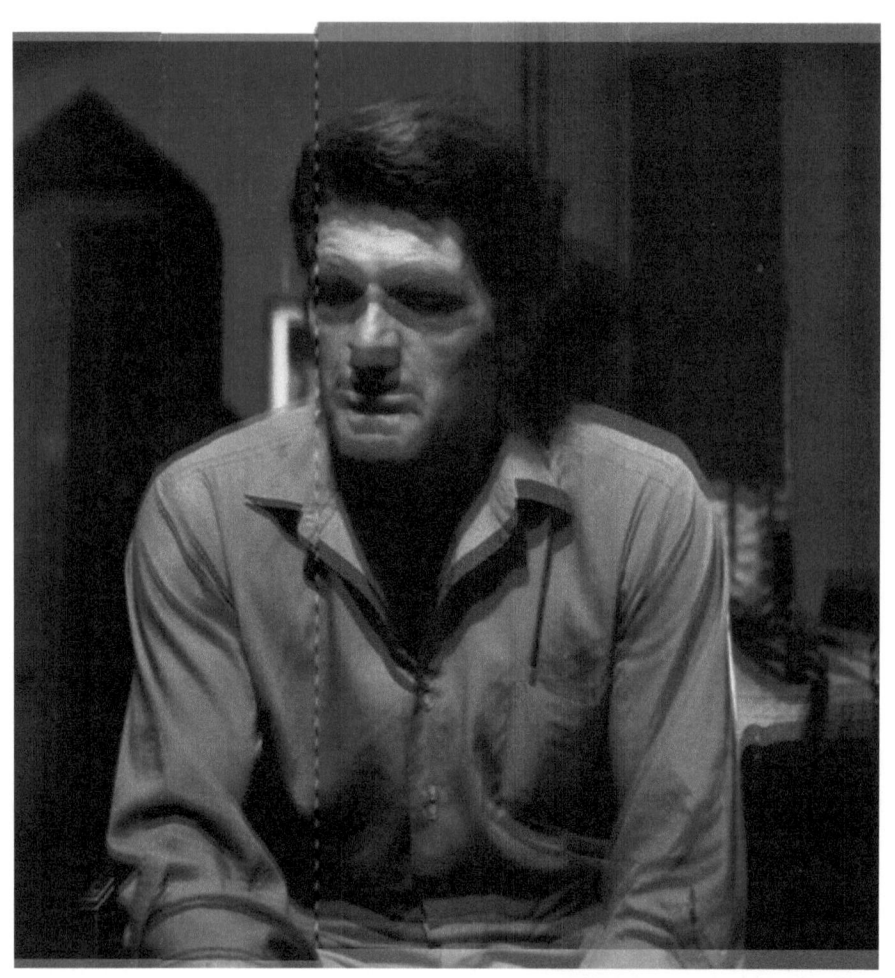
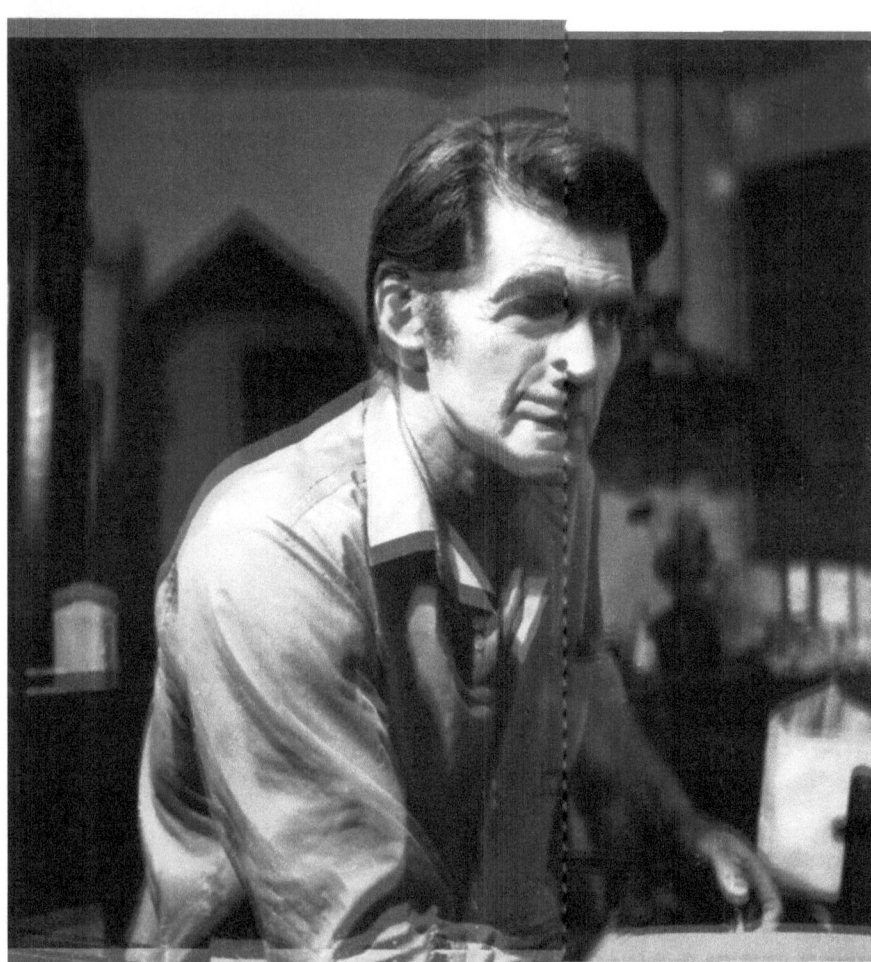

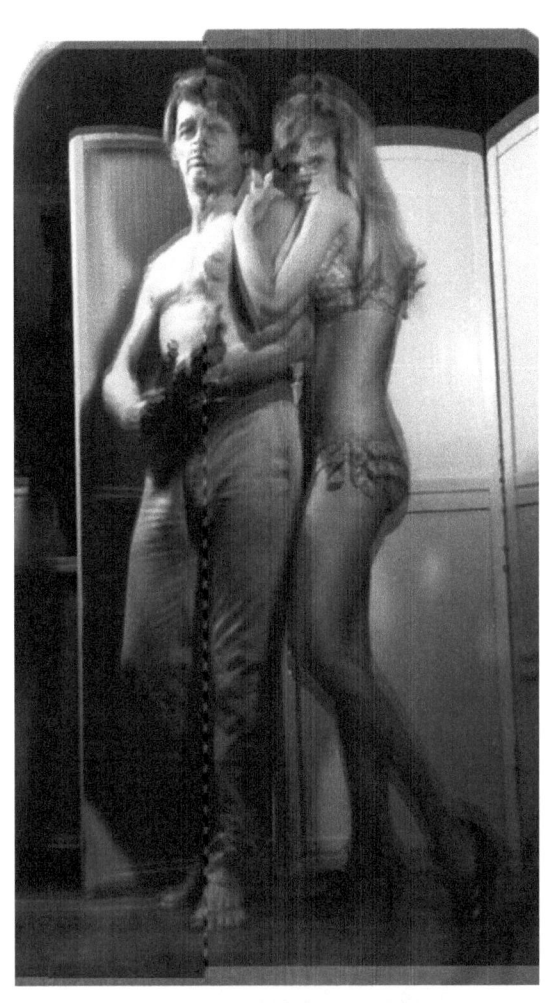
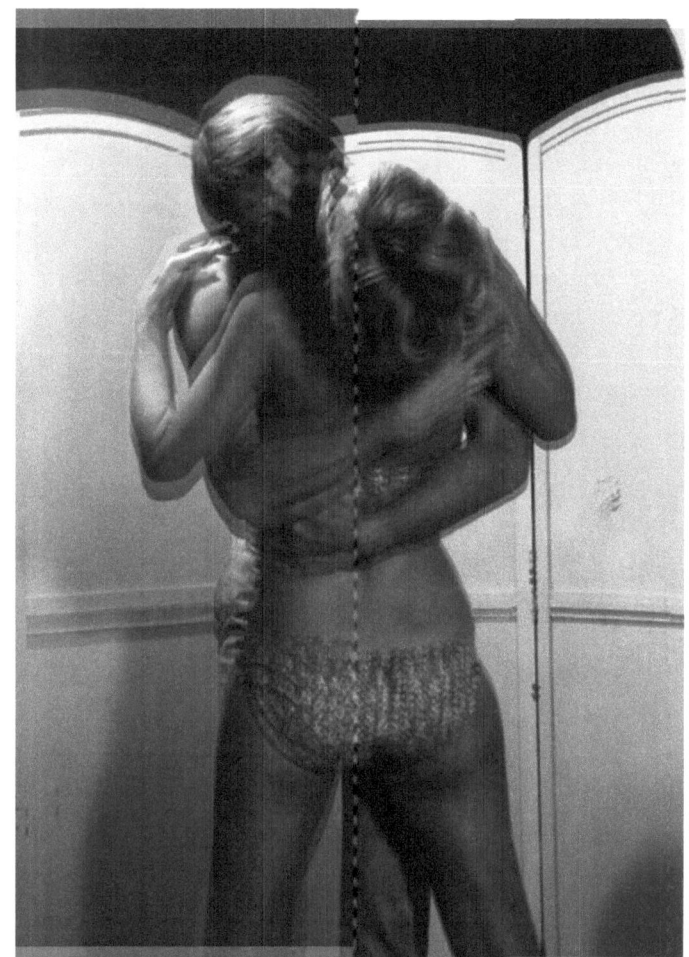
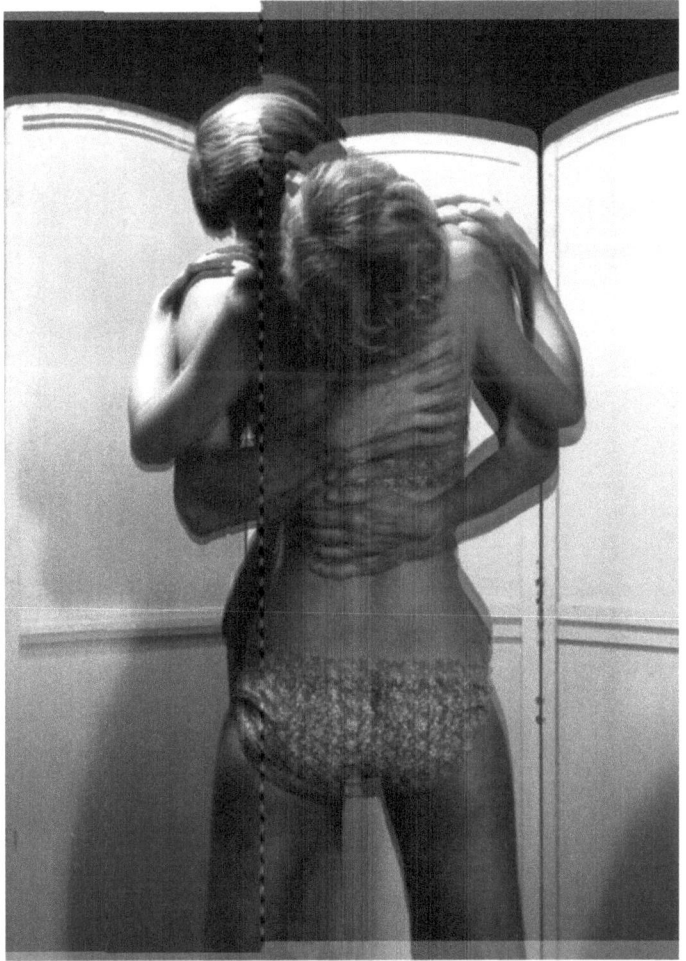
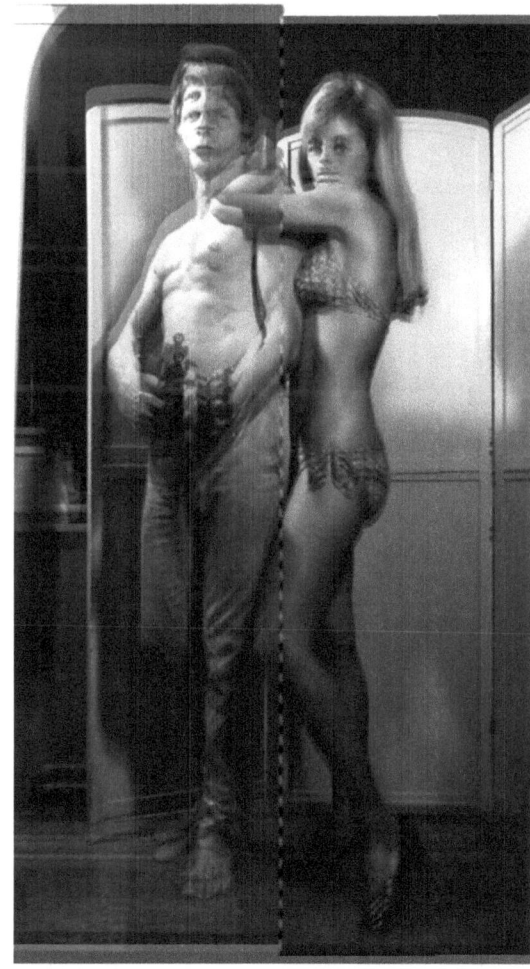

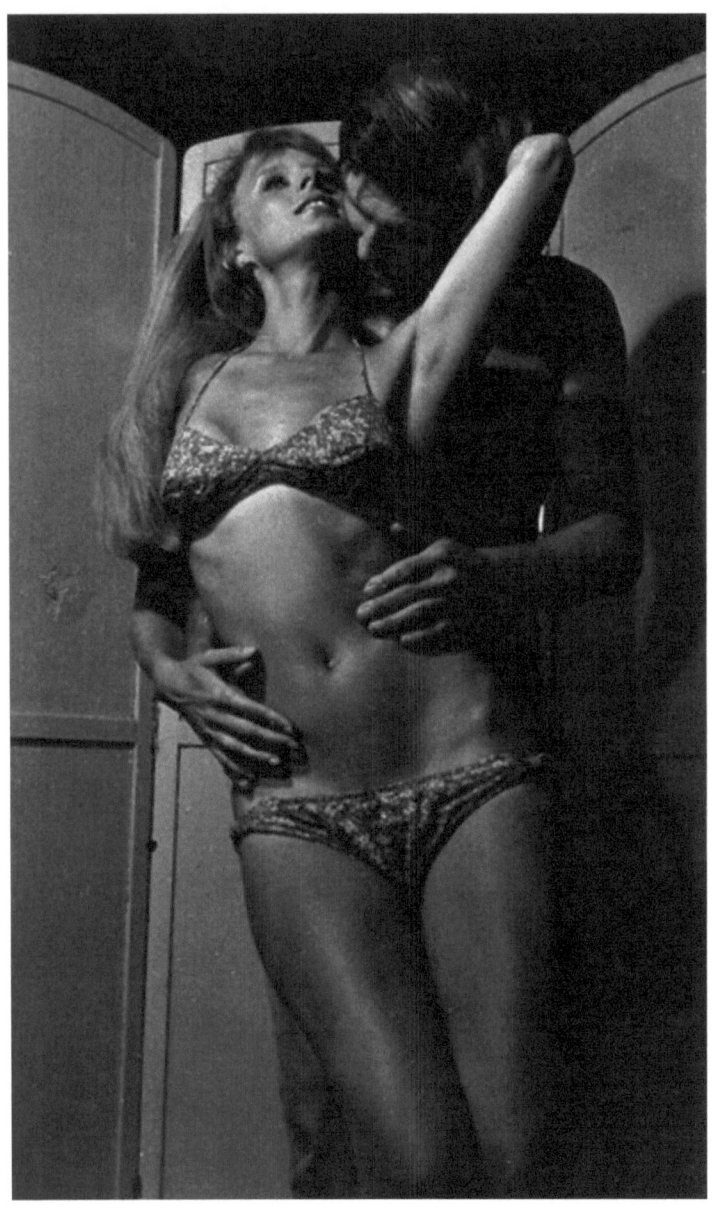
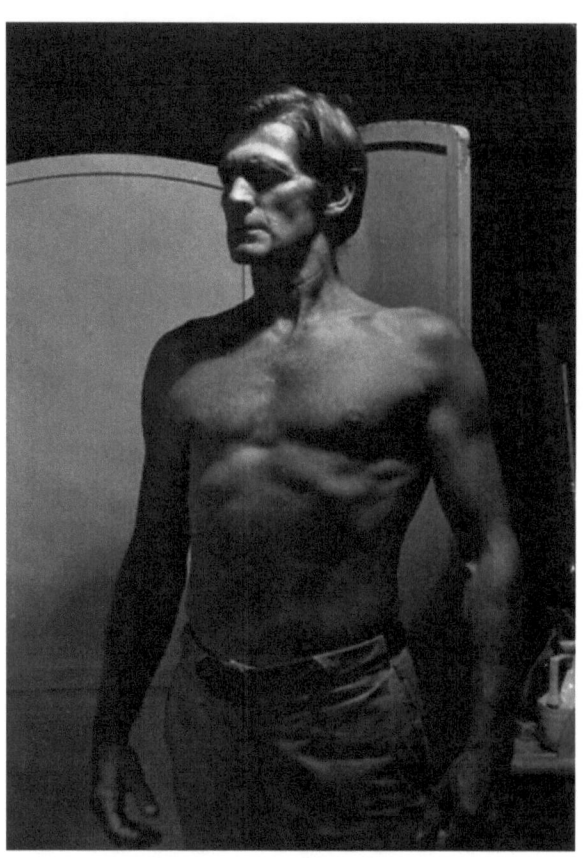
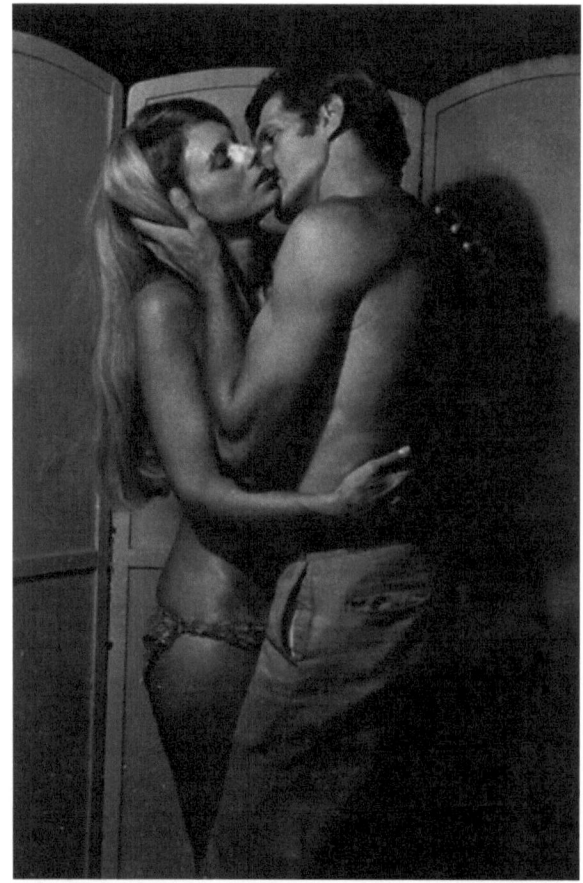

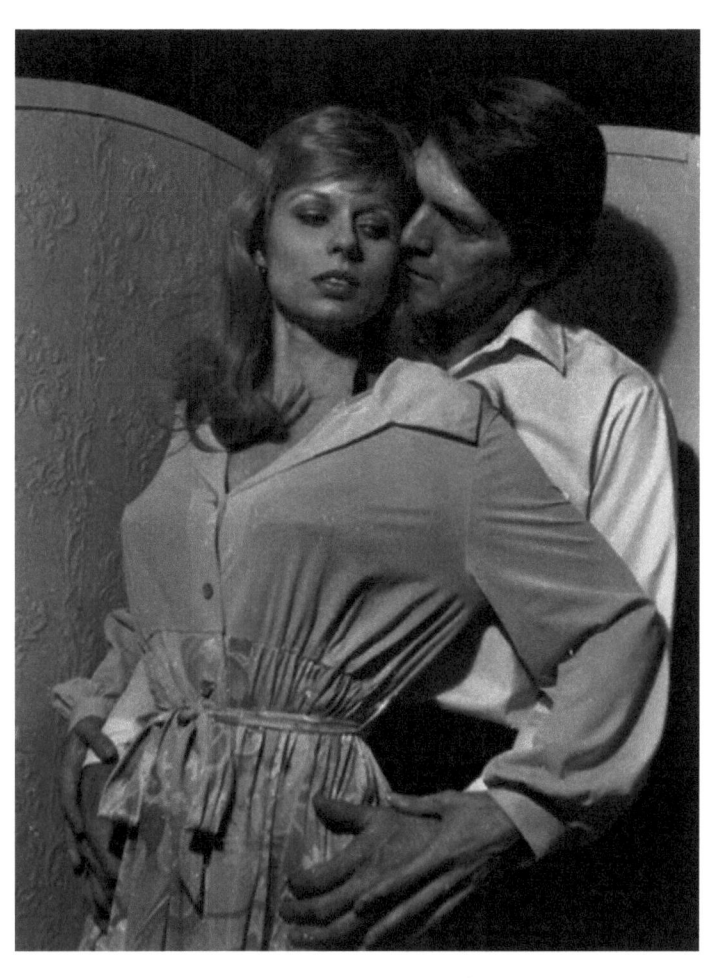
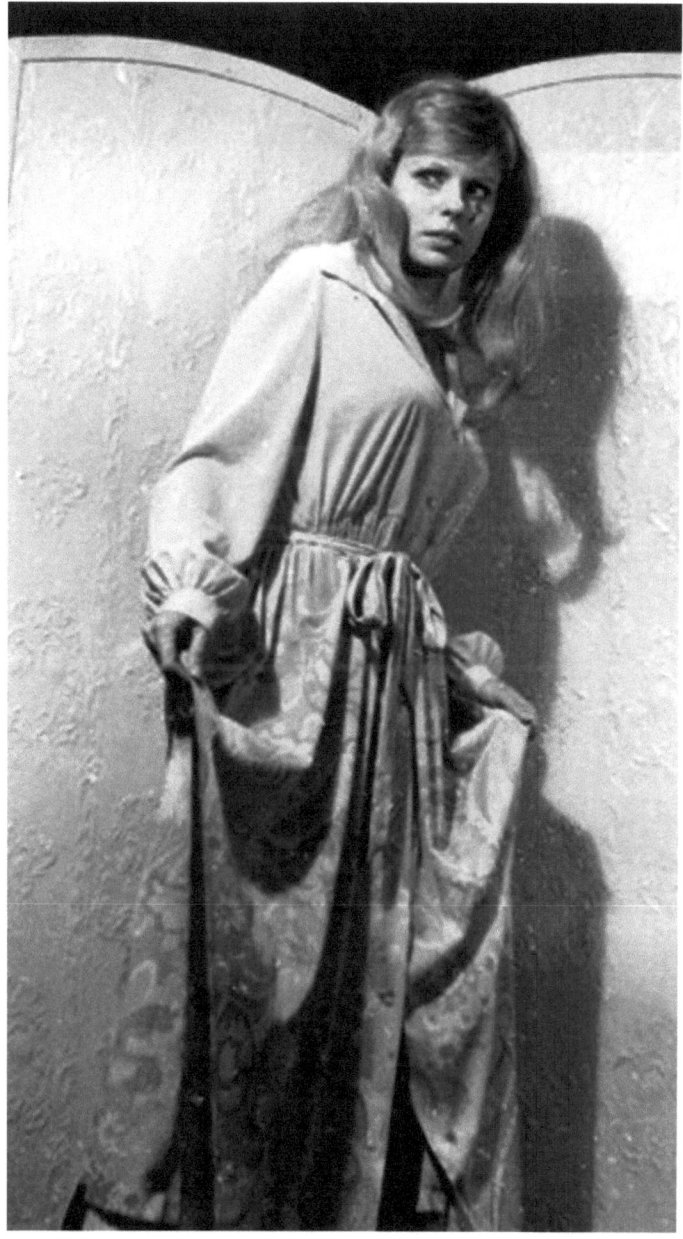

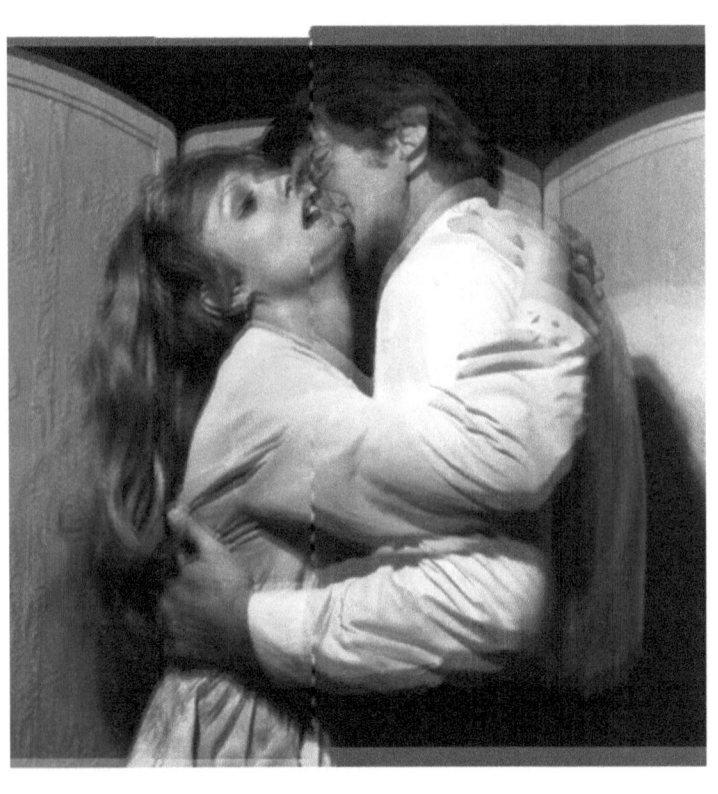
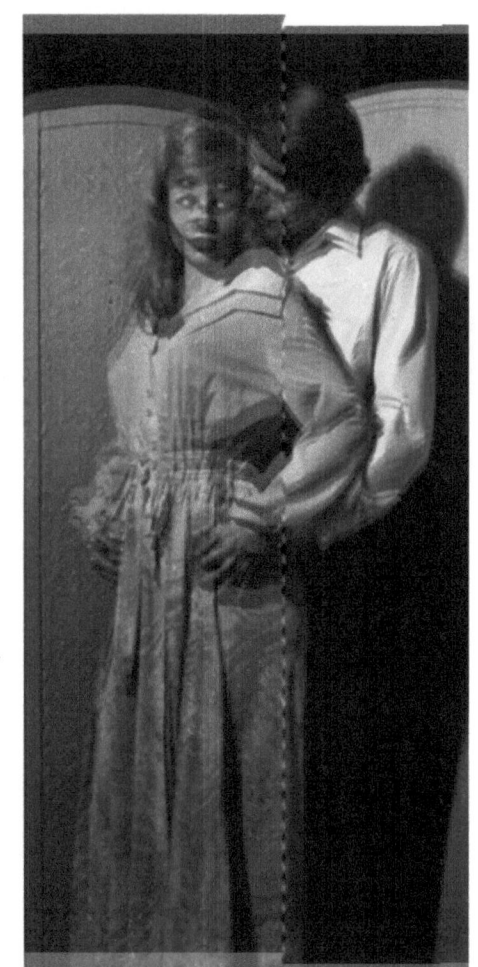
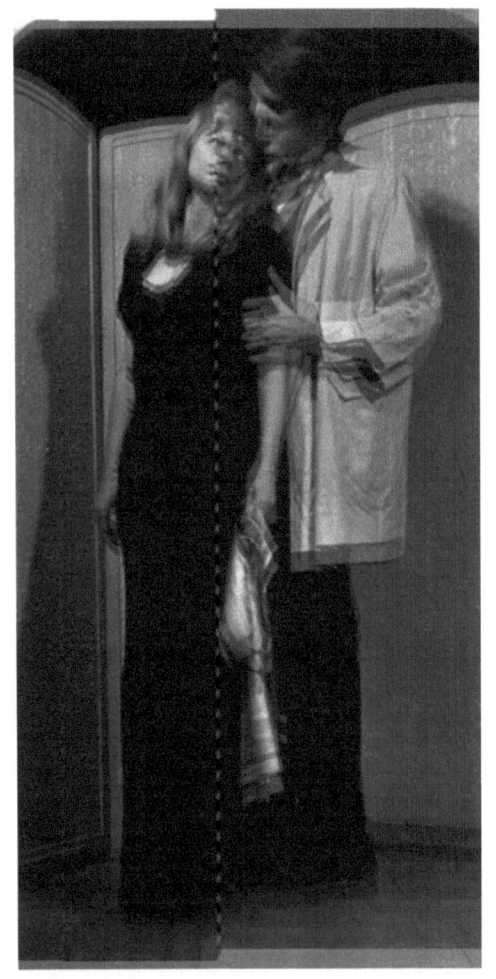
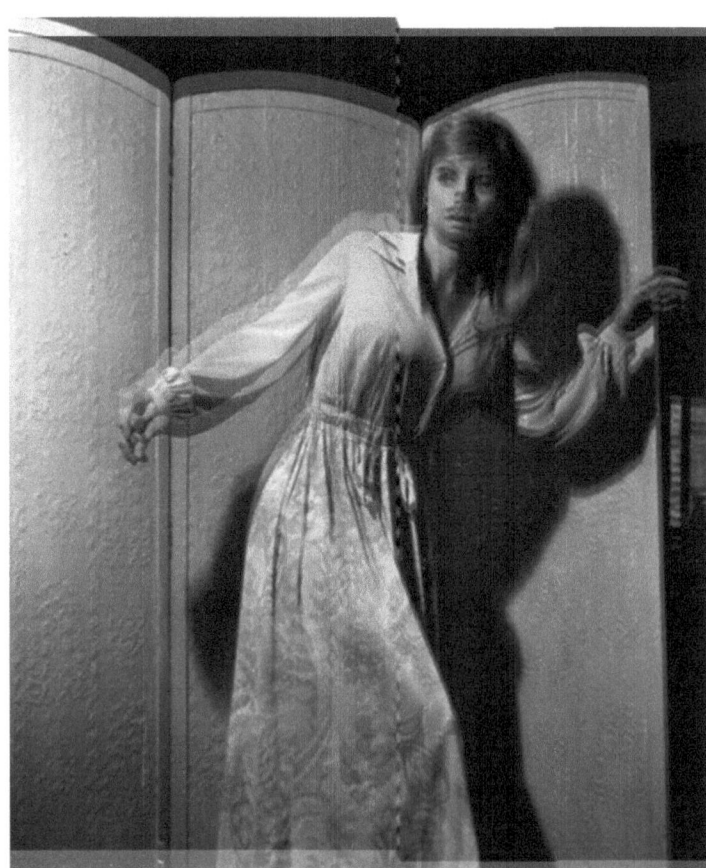

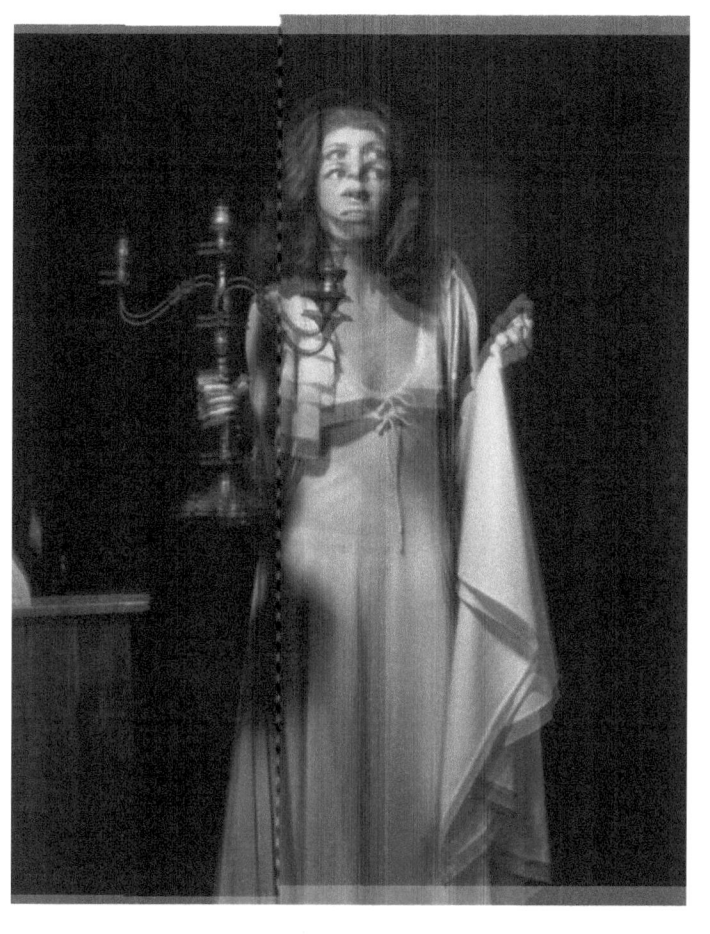
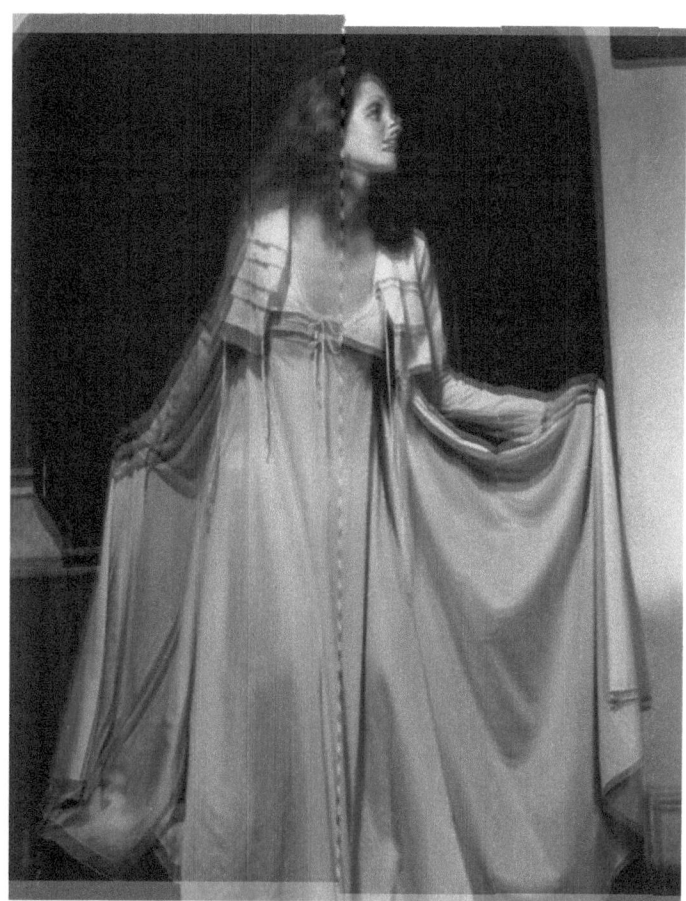
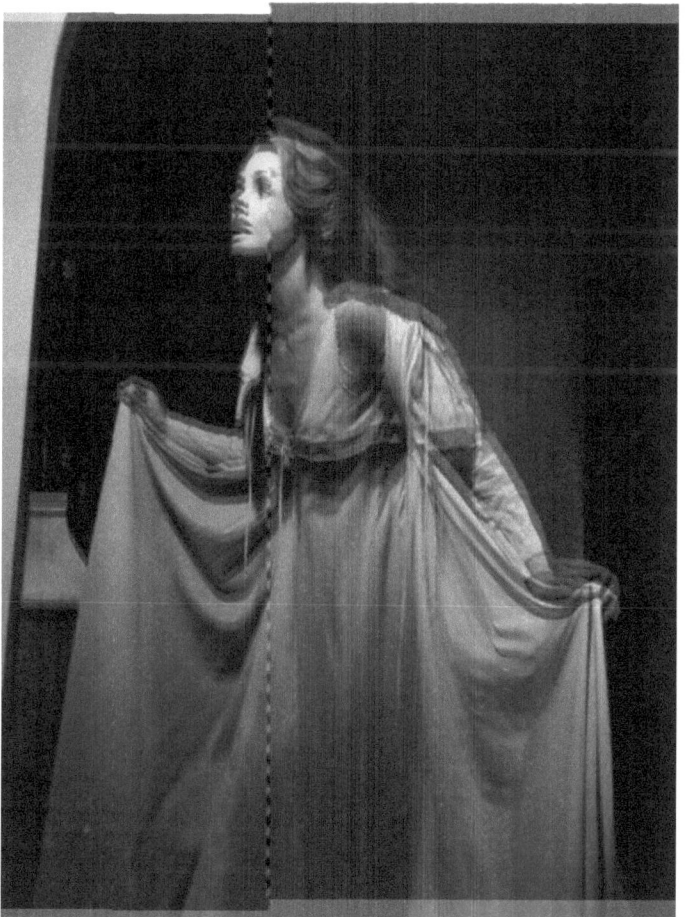
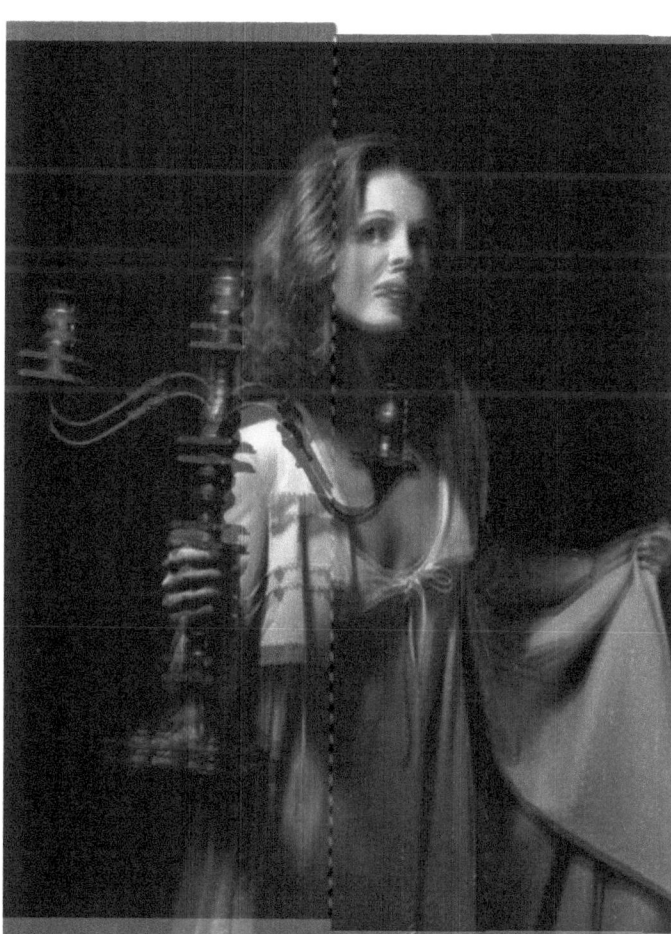

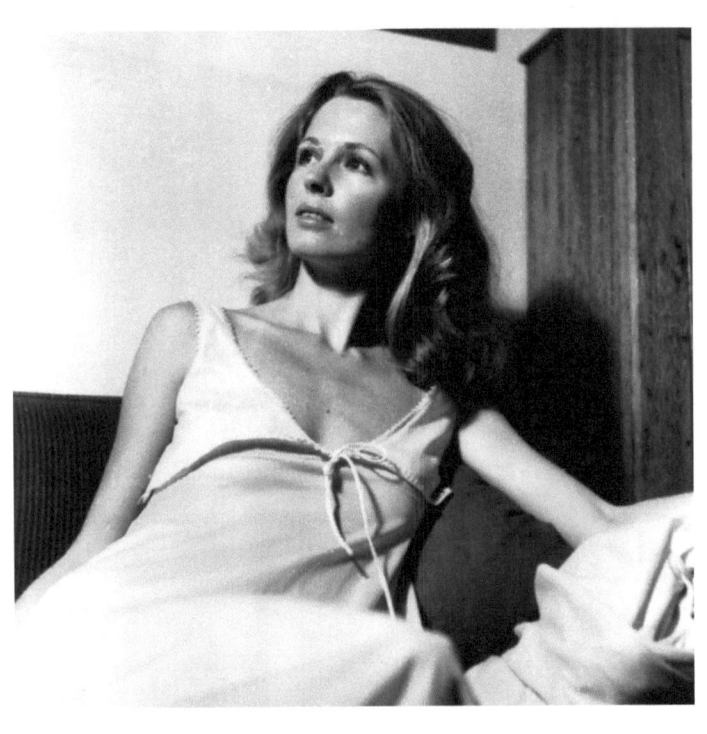
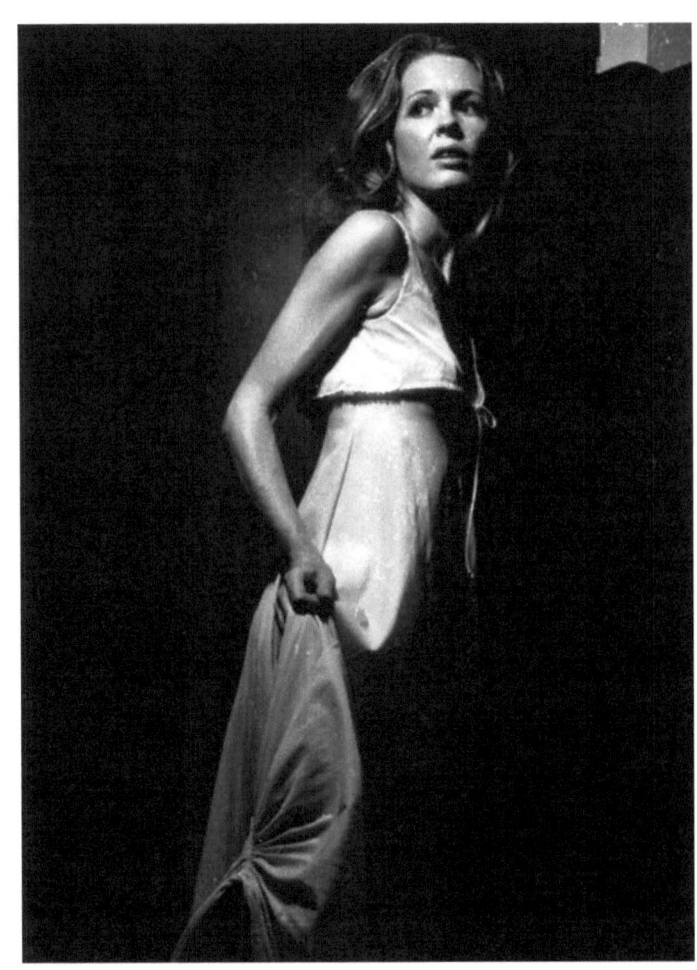
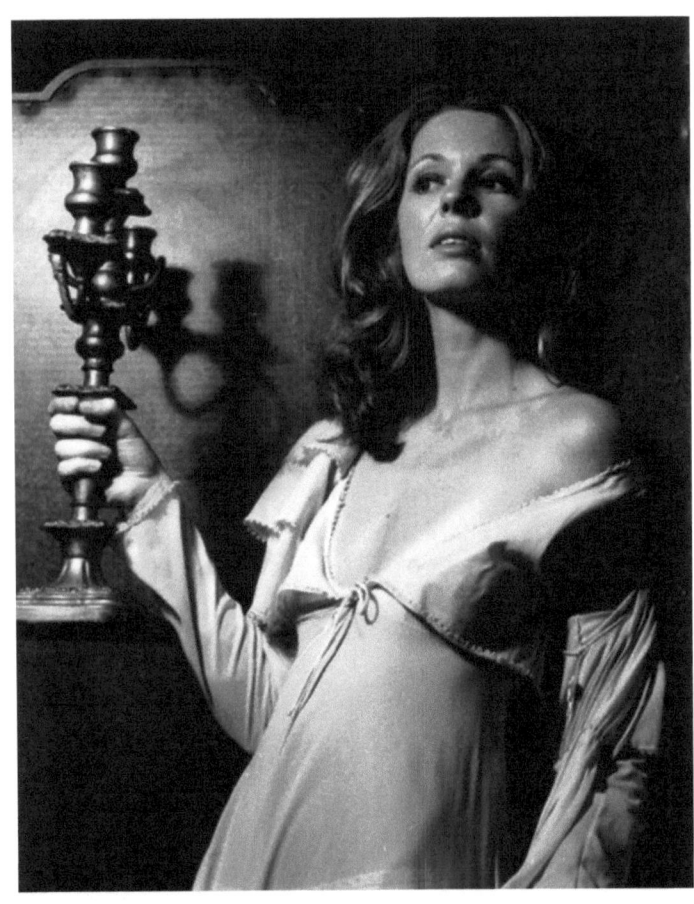
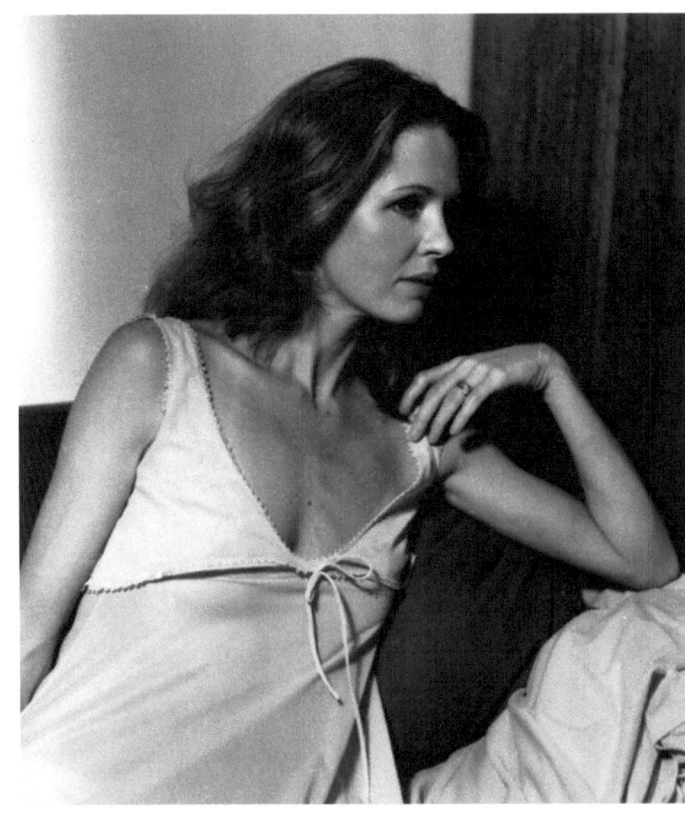

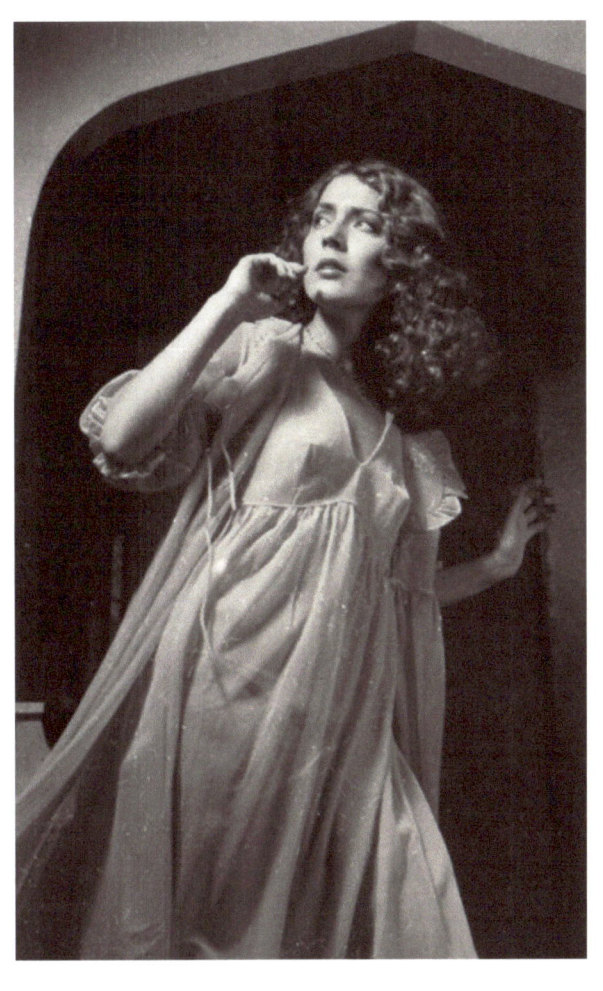
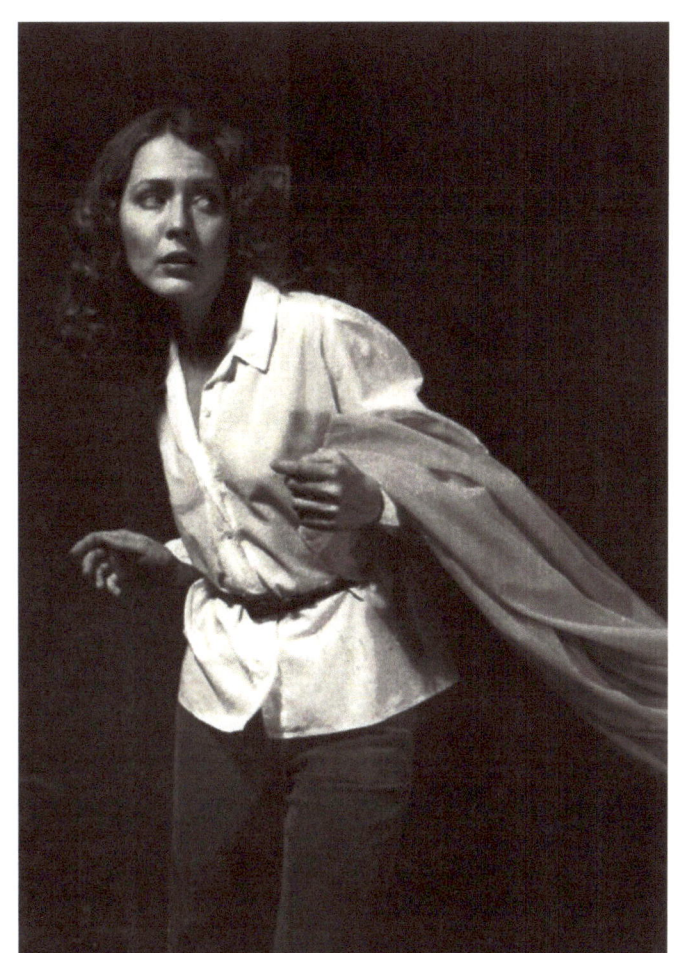
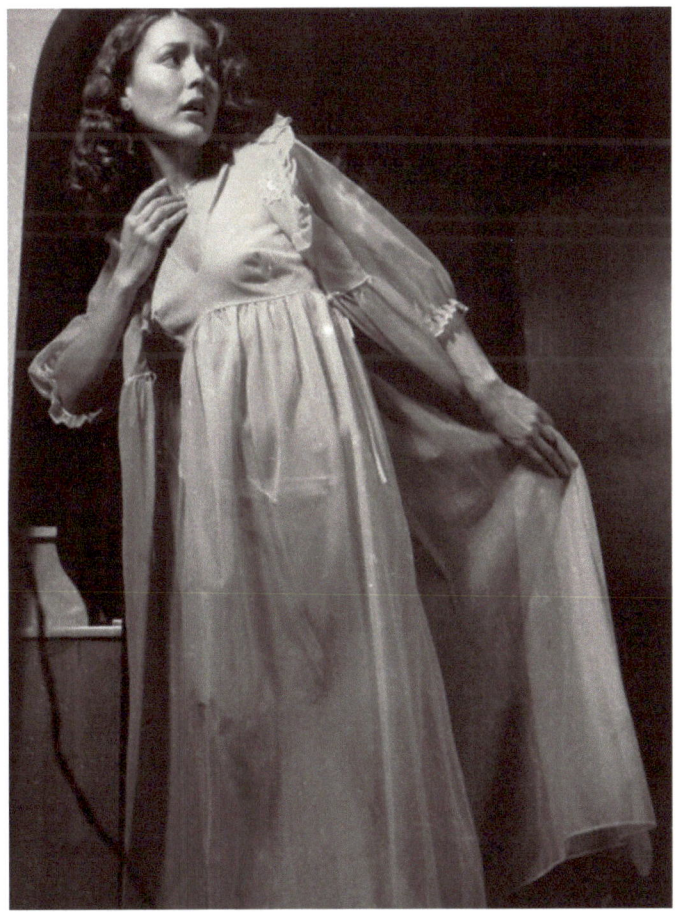
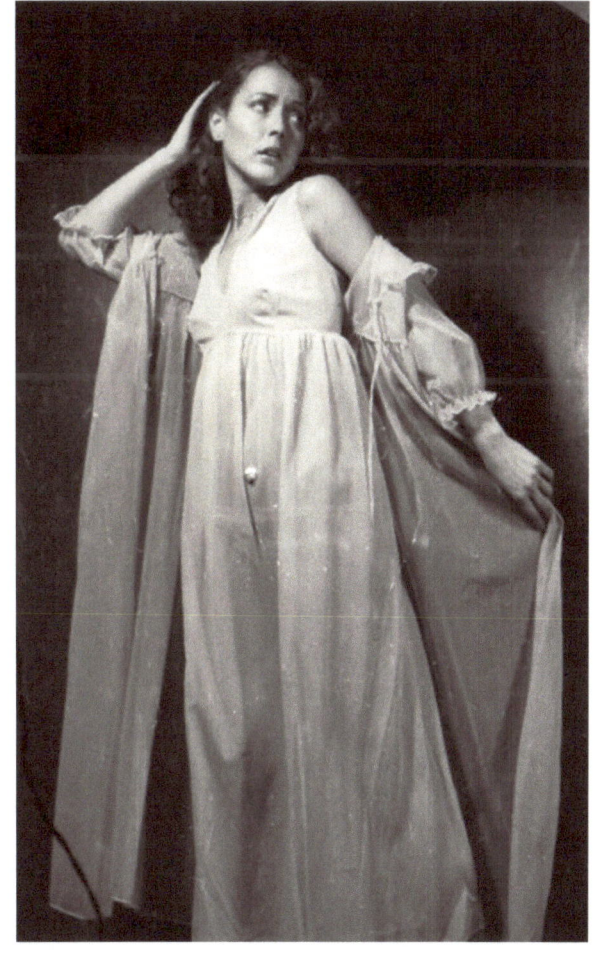

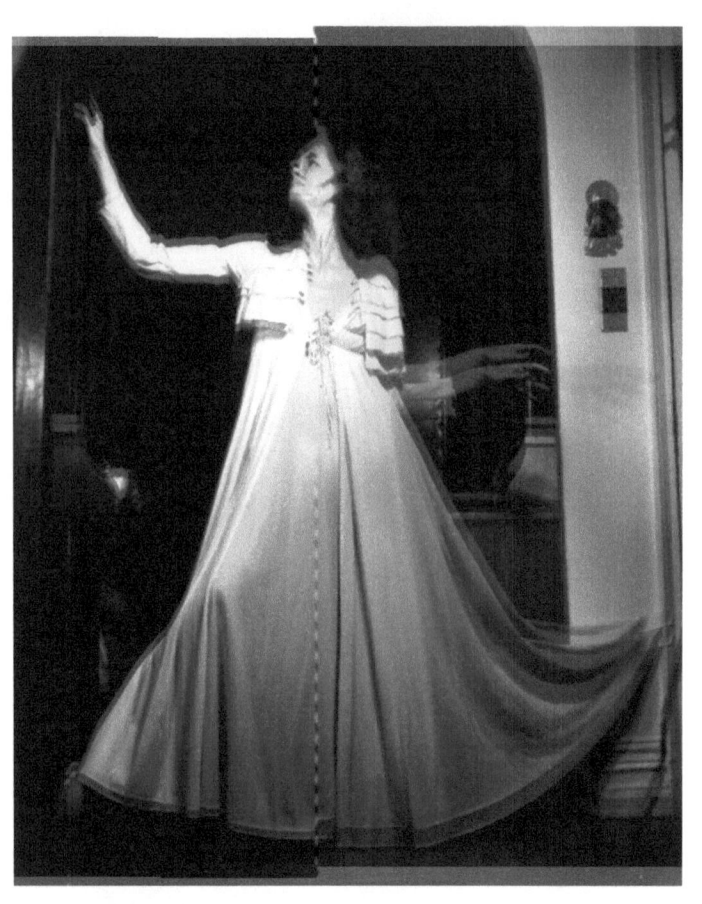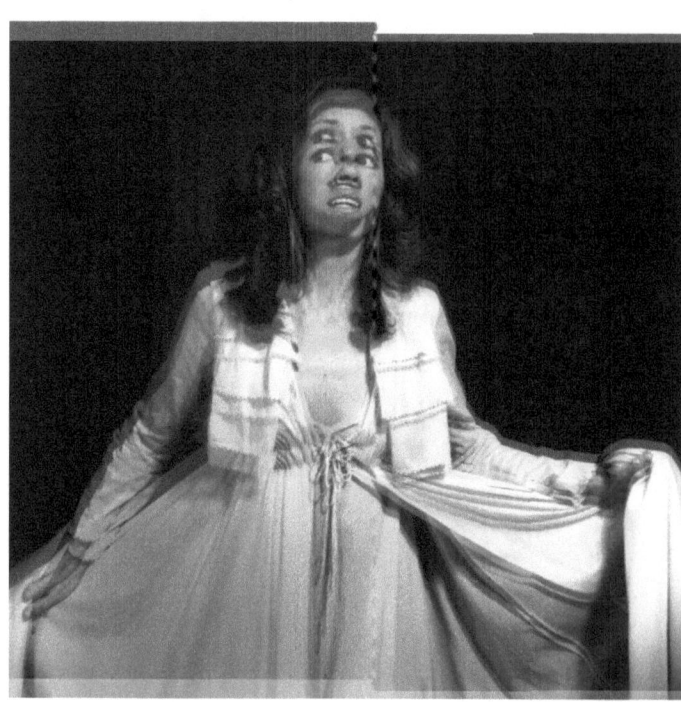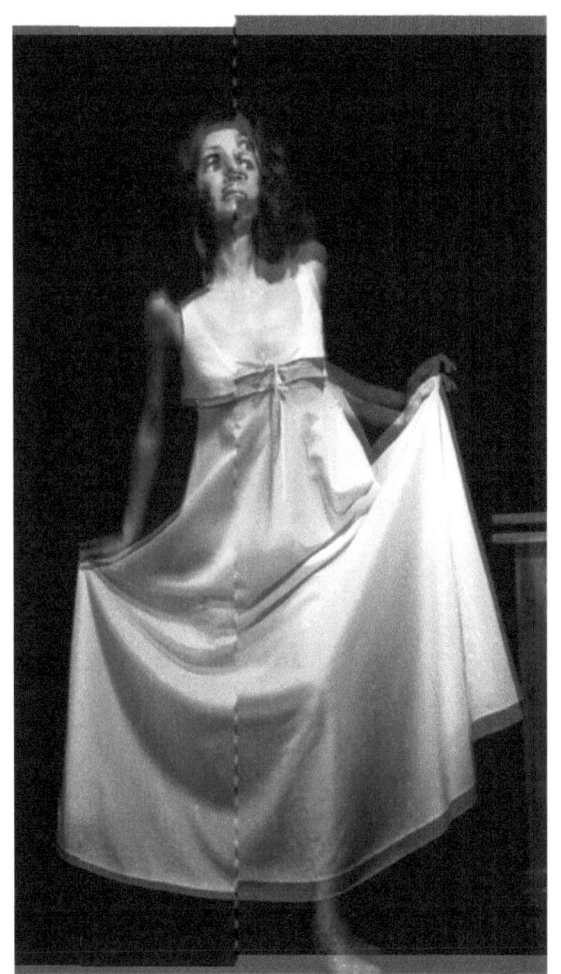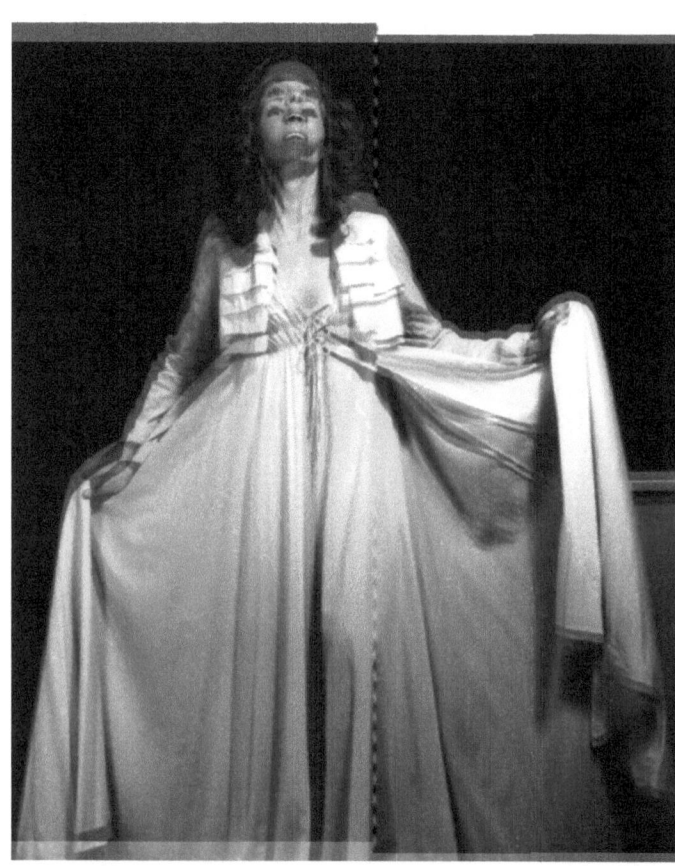

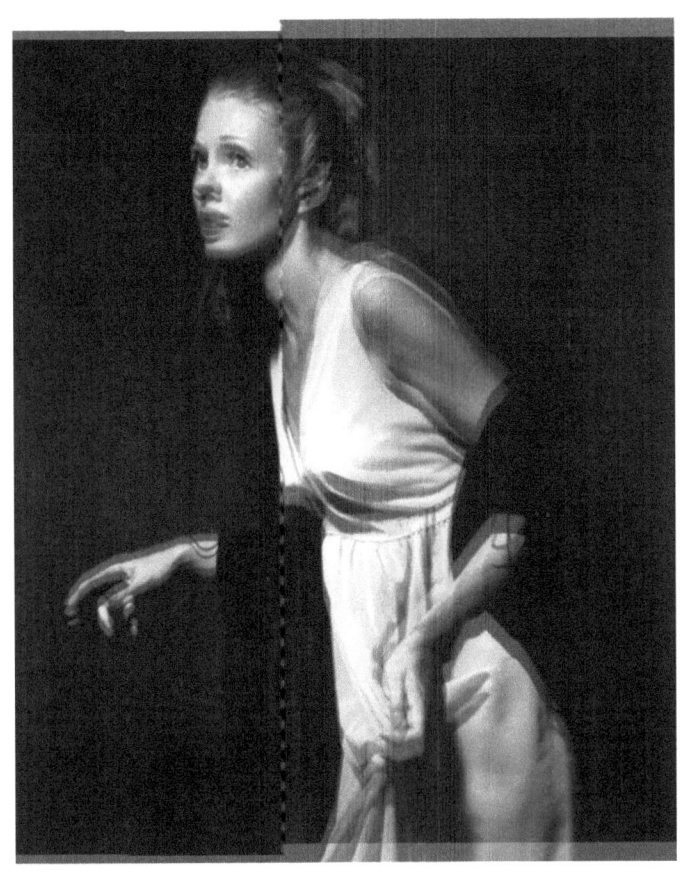
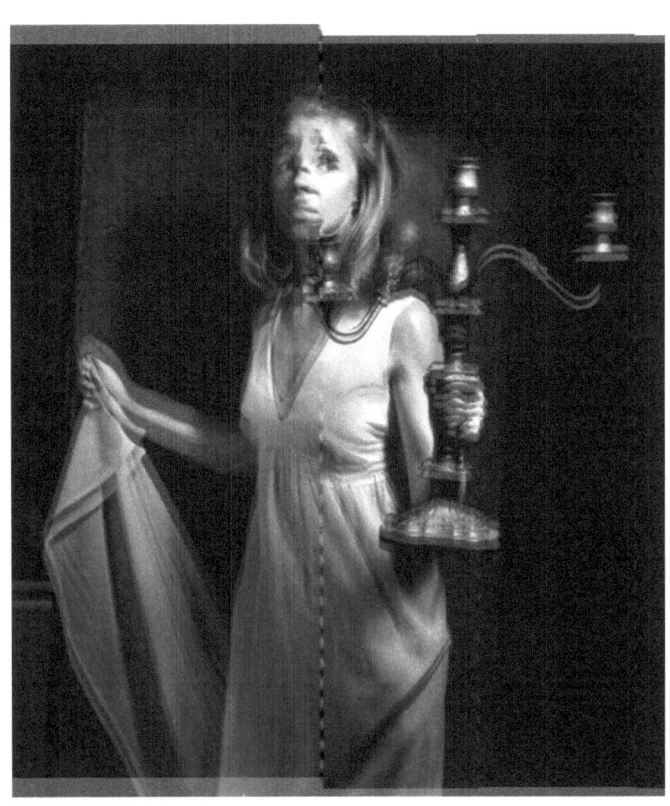
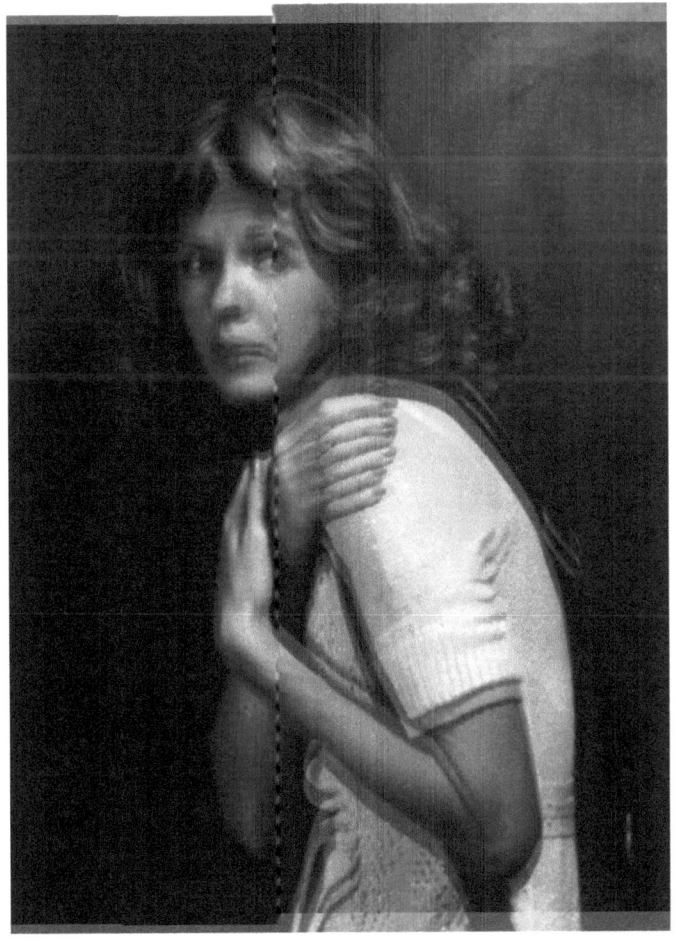
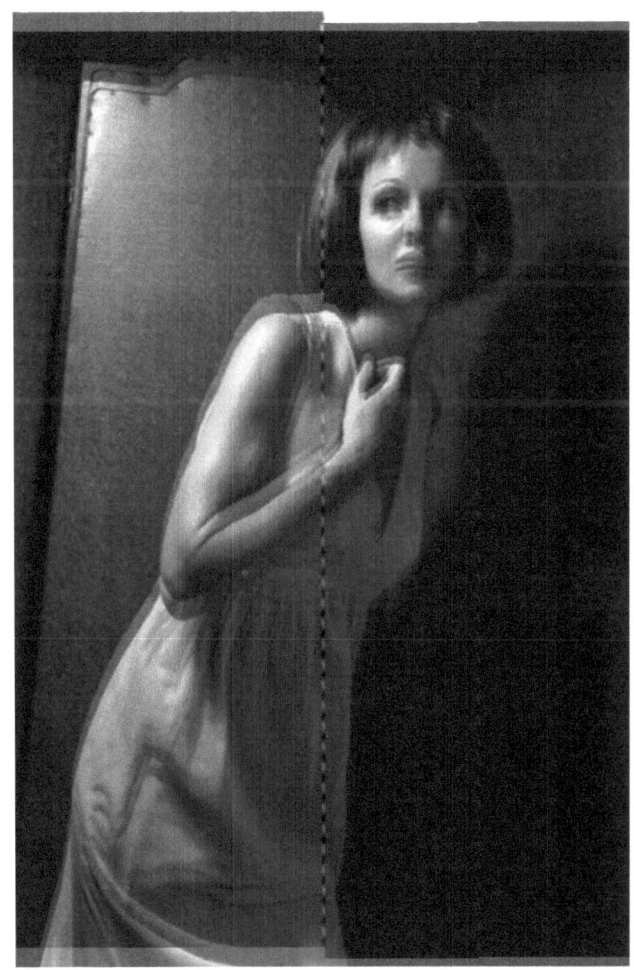

www.ingramcontent.com/pod-product-compliance
Lightning Source LLC
Chambersburg PA
CBHW051923210526
45473CB00006B/2116